ANGRYNOMICS

ANGRYNOMICS

Eric Lonergan and Mark Blyth

agenda
publishing

First published in 2020 by Agenda Publishing

Agenda Publishing Limited
The Core
Bath Lane
Newcastle Helix
Newcastle upon Tyne
NE4 5TF

www.agendapub.com

ISBN 978-1-78821-278-6 (hardcover)
ISBN 978-1-78821-279-3 (paperback)

British Library Cataloguing-in-Publication Data
A catalogue record for this book is
available from the British Library

Typeset by Patty Rennie

Printed and bound in the UK by TJ International

Contents

"A man is about as big as
the things that make him angry"
WINSTON CHURCHILL

Acknowledgements

A great many colleagues and friends have contributed to the thinking behind this book. Many of them will disagree with much of what follows. We have benefitted hugely from reading and discussing many of these ideas with Martin Wolf, Martin Sandbu, James Mackintosh, Adair Turner, Angus Armstrong, Roger Farmer, Carolina Alves, Anand Menon, Michael Burleigh, Frances Coppola, Daniel Mytnik, James Hanham, Simon Tilford, John Springford, Dave Fishwick, Jenny Rogers, Tony Finding, Tristan Hanson, Juan Nevado, Megan Greene, Simon Wren-Lewis, Kate Raworth, Roman Krznaric, Sony Kapoor, Alev Scott, Rupert Taylor, Clare Patey, Stewart Gilchrist, Nigel Kershaw, Kevin Riches, Matthias Matthijs, Jonathan Hopkin, Stephen Kinsella, Holly Goulet, Joe Hanrahan, Kimberly Witherspoon, Sarah Russo, Vicky Capstick, Rose McDermott, Carys Roberts, Wade Jacobi, John and Shelley Sawers and Matthew Lawrence.

Some of the policy ideas – such as dual interest rates – have been road-tested in the *Financial Times* and on Twitter. In the latter forum, we have greatly benefitted from the reflections of Brad Delong, David Andolfatto, Nick Rowe, Tony Yates, David Beckworth and Chris Dillow. Fran Boait and Stan Jourdan at the not-for-profit, Positive Money, have influenced our thinking on policy, as has Gregory Claeys at Bruegel. Steven Gerrard, at Agenda, has once again helped with great insight and care.

Eric would like to acknowledge his partner Corinne Sawers's intellect and sparkle, which has challenged and aided him at every turn. His daughters, Gina and Maia, are a constant inspiration, as is their nonna, Corinna Salvadori.

Mark would like to acknowledge his wife Jules steadfast refusal to engage with anything that he writes. Perhaps this book may prove the exception.

ERIC LONERGAN
MARK BLYTH

Introduction:
from economics to angrynomics

Strong societies can bounce back from a punch in the face. Consider Iceland. If the run up to the financial crisis of 2008 was a party, Iceland was party central. Four Icelandic banks went on a frenzied international expansion and grew their balance sheets (they bought stuff in the hope that it would go up in value) to ten times the size of the economy. When those banks went bust, they took the whole of Iceland's economy down with them. An epic punch in the face if ever there was one.

They may have been reckless, but Icelandic bankers and their co-workers had brains. When everything crashed, a lot of those brains went home and played video games – it's dark much of the time in Iceland. And then they hit on something. Online gaming is a global industry that requires a lot of computing power. Computing power makes heat. Heat needs to be cooled. So why not stick the servers for online gaming, Bitcoin mining, and a host of other things, in the ground in Iceland (the clue is in the name), and run the show from there? Which is what they did. Iceland had supportive institutions that didn't throw unemployed people under a bus, which allowed them to rethink their options and redeploy their capital.

The financial crisis hurt, to be sure, but given those institutions it also encouraged the growth of a whole new set of ideas and innovations that brought the country "most screwed" by the 2008 crisis back to its feet faster than almost all the others. By 2016, Iceland had fully recovered. Wages were higher than before the crisis, unemployment was low, and consumer confidence was high. Tourism was booming, in part because the crisis a decade earlier had crashed their currency, so it was a cheaper place to visit. Ten years later and the crisis seemed like a bad dream. Icelanders had never had it so good.

It was a different kind of punch in the face when in 2017 waves of angry protests broke out, and in greater numbers and with greater voice than any that had happened in 2008. That anger was triggered by revelations in the so-called "Panama Papers", which revealed tax dodging on an epic scale by Iceland's political and economic elites. The country that had suffered together through the crisis, had united for an improbably successful football run in the 2016 European Championships, had stuck by each other, and had come out ahead . . . suddenly got angry. "People came [to the protest] because they were so furious" said Jonas Haukdal, a Reykjavík ice-cream maker. "We thought we were over all that . . . we thought the scandals were behind us, that we knew what was ethical again. And then we find our prime minister has money offshore, and kept it quiet . . . It was like a betrayal."[1]

A similar story unfolded in France in 2018–19. Despite the weakening of austerity policies across Europe and growth returning to France, out of seemingly nowhere hundreds of thousands of WhatsApp-enabled "yellow jackets" took to the streets in protest. Ostensibly energized by a rise in the tax on diesel fuel, which hits poorer commuters especially hard, their demands expanded, and their networks spread beyond France, all based around a rejection of the cosy consensus engineered by their political elites. In 2019, the citizens of Hong Kong also rose in protest, as did the citizens of Chile, and for many of the same reasons – a disconnected elite, rising inequality and skewed advantage.

But this comes as no surprise. Neither that politicians lie, nor that ordinary people get angry at the disconnect between their lives and those of their elites. Indeed, we simply take it for granted that we live in an angry world. This is now the most conventional of all conventional wisdoms, the explanation for events the world over. "Oh, well people are very angry over in Germany, Austria, France, the United States, the UK, Indonesia, Hong Kong...". Not only is seemingly everyone angry, but everyone assumes that we understand why – that anger is obvious. But is it? Is all anger the same? Why *anger*, and not passion, or fear, energy, or optimism? In *Angrynomics* we are seeking to make sense of what appears at first sight to be an incoherent outpouring of a primitive emotion.

When economics becomes angrynomics

To understand what "angrynomics" is, let's first start with economics. Economics is a set of ideas, a map, that tells us how the world of markets and exchange works. It is also a description of the world in which we live. If the world of economic theory, the map, accurately describes the terrain in which we live, then it's a good map. Are these economic maps any good? That's an open question. In the very few bits of the world where economic theory is directly applied, for example in central bank forecasting departments, highly complex models of the economy called dynamic stochastic general equilibrium (DSGE) models are populated by what are called "representative agents". These "agents" are supposed to be people, but they are strangely ageless, sexless, tasteless, non-ideological, and they live forever.

In this emotionless and timeless world, "the economy" is nothing more than the number of workers, multiplied by the number of hours worked, plus the amount of capital (machines, technology, etc.) that they work with. That's it. There's no politics, no concern over who gets what and why. As these fictitious economies mature, they accumulate more capital and all the agents get richer, and as they do, they work less. This is a very comforting world, but is it the world in which most of us actually live? Does the map mirror the territory?

In the world we inhabit, it appears both true that society as a whole has never been richer, and yet most of us seem to be working more. As for the distribution of income, the Federal Reserve Bank of St. Louis describes how in its model "the last workers to be hired by a business should receive pay that is equal to their contribution to the output of that business".[2] This sounds pretty reasonable. But this doesn't seem to mirror reality, either. CEO pay has rocketed to hundreds of times that of employees, many of whom have not had a pay increase for decades, when you adjust for inflation. Clearly power matters here, but power is nowhere to be found in our modeled world. Indeed, the distribution of wealth has not just become extreme, but politics has become the playground of those with vast wealth. Billionaires spend millions protecting their interests, or supporting their personal, often eccentric, agendas – such as secretive hedge fund managers bankrolling the Brexit campaign.[3]

Economics is a powerful map of the world. But the map that we have been working with for the past 30 plus years – what the economist Dani Rodrik calls "the neoliberal map" – works in theory, in models, but increasingly fails to describe what most of us experience and care about. That is, a world of seemingly ever-tighter budgets, ever-rising costs (despite being constantly told that there is no inflation), and ever-increasing stresses in and beyond the work place. At some point, the disconnect between our experience of the world and the model used to explain it has to come to a head.

Economics as it stands can't seem to explain why the pressures of life appear to be intensifying, at the same time as income per capita is rising. Nor can it explain why pensioners, whose incomes depend upon the number of workers in work paying taxes, reject immigration more than any other group, when they forgot to have enough kids to keep it all going? Why do we see the rise of nationalism everywhere when we hear that globalization, on average, has made us all richer? One part of that answer lies in this disconnect between what is assumed to be going on in our models and what is actually happening in the world as it is. A second part lies in another disconnect, which is the inauthenticity of the elites pursuing steady progress in "GDP per capita" to the rest of us who witness dramatic and disconcerting societal change.

Elites are nothing new. It used to be the case that political elites were defined by *who* they represented. Labour and social democratic parties represented the interests of workers while conservative and liberal parties represented the interests of business. By the 1990s those relationships began to breakdown and a new politics emerged throughout the developed world where such "left" and "right" divisions were increasingly thought to be arcane and irrelevant relics of the Cold War. In its place emerged a new politics where politicians ceased to represent core constituencies and instead sought to capture a so-called "median voter" who acted like the representative agent in our economic models.

These voters cared not for economic conflict, but supposedly cared for post-materialist values and good governance, which parties duly agreed to supply. The big policy stuff was best left to experts in international organizations and independent central banks. Politicians supplied less policy and yet pretended to represent everyone's interests while doing so.[4] This was the world of the 1990s and 2000s, wonderfully described as "the Great Moderation" in 2004 by then Federal Reserve Chair Ben Bernanke, whereby the elimination of politics at the hands of technocrats had delivered prosperity for all.[5] There were, as we know now, rather large flaws with this view of the world.

Chief among them was that material concerns never went away. Parties simply stopped admitting that they existed. The UK economy doubled in size from 1980 to 2017. Over the same period use of food banks increased 1000 per cent. In much of the developed world, inequality rose throughout the 1980s and 1990s, dipped for a decade, and shot up again after the financial crisis. Over the same period global corporations simply stopped paying taxes. The same elites that confused the real world for the world in their economic models lost their credibility with the voters that they portrayed themselves as representing.

Then came Iraq, dodgy-dossiers, 45 minutes claims, and Afghanistan – the war without end. Followed by the celebration of finance as the engine of growth, which blew up in our faces and which was swiftly followed by state funded bailouts to save the assets of the already rich. A bailout paid for by the already squeezed with the shift to austerity policies that in some cases saw 30 per cent cuts in local services.[6] Meanwhile in the metropoles, banks went back to earning billions and house prices worked like magic ATMs.

When politicians really needed to motivate electorates, they stopped making the case for deep-rooted economic change, and reverted to fear. In the euro crisis, populations were held in check by threats of renewed financial panic. In both the Scottish independence and Brexit referendums, the threat of losing what you have was used as a weapon to defend the status quo. Across central and eastern Europe, fear of migrants destroying "our" culture became the motivating meme.

You can't expect real people – neither synthetic representative agents nor imaginary median voters – to put up with these disconnects forever. Eventually the gap between how we experience the world and the economic model used by elites to explain and justify it becomes too large to ignore and self-serving elites get called out. Welcome to that calling, the world of "angrynomics", where real people are angry and have every reason to be.

Thinking and living in an angrynomics world

Anger, the most powerful human emotion, has become the arc that connects the dry, statistical world described by technocrats, policy wonks and politicians with the world as we experience it. Economics becomes angrynomics when on a macro level the system crashes and exposes the faultlines that have been covered up for so long.

This book explores how our political economy has given rise to anger: public anger, both moral outrage and tribal rage, and private anger. Together these forms of anger help us to understand the themes in this book. If economics describes the way the economy is supposed to work, angrynomics reveals what we actually experience, and why it matters to us. It helps us to make sense of global politics, tells us what to listen to, what to be beware of, and how we might seek to fix a broken economy.

The first distinction that we make is between public and private anger. Much research treats the two as equivalent, but in fact they are opposites. Public anger is often worn like a badge of honour. Icelanders protesting against a corrupt political class are emboldened by virtue. They railed against corruption and sought moral redress. Extinction Rebellion is fueled by the anger of righteousness. When people are publicly angry, because they are wronged, or they witness wrong-doing, they want it to be recognized and addressed. This is moral outrage.

Private anger resembles its opposite. It is often characterized by shame. People who are angry in their private lives, often seek counseling, rather than retribution. An angry colleague, a stressed parent, or an enraged driver – these are people in need of help, not deserving of redress.

But public anger itself is also two-sided. If moral outrage is its positive form, reinforcing and generating tribal identity is its opposite. Tribal rage is a primitive emotion, one that puts aside our moral compass in the name of action and to close ranks for protection against some other group. Think of a local derby match between fierce rivals. Chances are you'll see an angry minority. Why are they there? Because they are the truest of fans. They wear their badge of loyalty aggressively. Indeed not only do they threaten the opposition fans or players, they can as easily turn on their own, demanding greater loyalty and commitment. Angry fans regulate their *own* tribe.

Moral outrage, the positive face of public anger, seeks redress. It is a call to be listened to, that enough is enough, and a wrong must be righted. But in its contrasting form, tribal anger seeks to threaten in order to dominate, suppress, and at its most violent, to destroy. Seen this way, the different types of public anger serve different functions: to enforce ethical norms and to regulate tribal identity. This is how anger and the economy become combined. Today, cynical politicians effortlessly play on both forms of anger to garner support. By using these notions of public and private anger, of moral outrage and tribal energy, we can better understand the actions of politicians and identify what to resist. The challenge for politics today is to listen carefully to, and redress, the legitimate anger of moral outrage while exposing and not inciting, the violent anger of tribes.

Whereas public forms of anger often take the form of a proud expression of moral legitimacy or tribal allegiance, private anger is associated with internal struggle. The root causes of private anger – increased personal anxiety, stress, insecurity, and our feelings of powerlessness in the face of apparently inevitable external change – are tied to the micro- and macro-economic trends and economic outcomes that we discuss in this book. Specifically, we argue that while rapid economic and technological change may be necessary to deliver growth in productivity and output to address environmental, social and demographic needs, the transition and disruption to get there creates stress, anxiety, and something that humans are particularly bad at dealing with: uncertainty.

We don't like living with uncertainty and try as much as possible to minimize it. But the economy that we have built over the past 30 years demands that we embrace it, at the same time as governments have progressively abandoned their commitments to provide their citizens with protection from it. Combine that with a world where the maps guiding our actions seem to be both less accurate and decidedly skewed to the interests of an entrenched elite, and we shift from economics as imagined to angrynomics in practice.

The threat we feel from rapid and seemingly ever-accelerating economic change means that listening to private and public anger is critical to a deeper understanding of what we actually experience in our daily lives, and how to address those anxieties. A fundamental tension is clear. Aging societies such as ours need more technology, not less. It is not to be feared. It is to be embraced. Prosperity is increased by innovation which augments productivity. Innovation is the root cause of material advancement and it increases our collective resources. Unfortunately, it also gives us Instagram. Change can be exciting, particularly for the immediate beneficiaries, or those with little to lose. But for most people it is disconcerting if not frightening. Most of us crave security, stability and certainty. When rapid changes are accompanied by real income losses, or we perceive that one person's gain is another's loss, quite reasonably, we get angry. This expresses itself in both moral outrage – that the wrong be righted – and in tribalism – as we seek to blame the "other" that must be responsible.

Recognizing this core dilemma – how to profit from uncertainty while hating it – is a precondition for progress in making us all less angry so that we can seriously address the social, economic and environmental challenges of our time. We think that with the right approach to this simple fact of life we can live longer, be healthier, and perhaps even be happier. But to do that we need to shift our perspective from economics to understanding angrynomics: an economy of heightened uncertainty and anger, where faith in the workings of markets and politics has been undermined. We explain why this has happened and what to do about it.

Why read this book and what's unusual about it?

This book is written not for our academic and professional colleagues. They will find the lack of footnotes and the lack of "rigour" unsettling. Moreover, it is written as a dialogue between the two authors, which is decidedly unscholarly. We also think the system is broken. We do not think that the current order can be "nudged" back into stability. And simply going back to the politics of the early 2000s is not, and should not, be an option. Neither is a return to the 1970s.

As we elaborate later in the book, we think of capitalism as a computer that has just had a massive crash. However, only a small software patch was installed to get it up and running again when what it really needs is a whole new operating system. Populism – of the left and right – is a recognition of that. Populists are the rogue code-writers of politics that thrive on anger. Unfortunately, they are shitty programmers. We hope to motivate the search for a better operating system.

Angrynomics is here and now. It is determining elections. It is recasting party politics across the world – not just Trump and Brexit, but in countries as diverse as Germany, Brazil and Ukraine, and in the revival of nationalism in Hungary and Poland, Russia's foreign policy, Turkey's growing anti-Europeanism, and in the collapse of traditional centre parties everywhere. We see anger at the stressors we are all exposed to being hijacked by the media and political classes to detrimental ends. Tribalism – and its regulating energy, anger – is a natural reflex, but it is always based upon myths and is ultimately self-defeating.

Our job here is to help understand the anger that is driving this moment, while exposing and disarming its cynical manipulation which drives so much of our politics today. This book is an attempt to see why the world is acting the way it is, and to suggest what we might do about it. Yet we don't want to stop at diagnosis. We want to reduce the anger. And we think that the key to doing so is to advocate for radical new policies, and indeed a new politics, that cuts across tired political lines and addresses the huge economic and political challenges directly.

We have tried to write a book that has some of the force and dynamic of anger itself, so what follows is a series of *Dialogues*, not Chapters. Conversation allows us to engage and disagree, rather than lecture. An open exchange is not a settled debate. Rather, we are inviting the reader to be a part of our conversation and to be free to make up their own mind about what we are saying. Discussion, we feel, better allows us to explain in as accessible way as possible what we think are the issues and what we think can be done about them. Each dialogue begins with a "parable" that we hope illuminates the problem and suggests where we are going with it.

This book is also short, and it is intended to be. Indeed, it doesn't need to be read from cover to cover. Dialogue 3, for example, leaves the present and puts our current angry world into historical context – it is a whirlwind tour of 70 years of political economy. You can jump straight there if you want to know how the global economy works – all explained in 30 minutes reading! Or you can skip it if you're not too keen on economics and prefer to stay with the politics. But we hope that you do stick with the economics. Just as war is too important to be left to the generals, so economics is too important to be left to just economists, especially when it has morphed into angrynomics. What we hope to show through these dialogues is that much of what we think about the future, and why we are angry, is misplaced. People have every right to be pissed off – as the British say – but please, be pissed off about the right things. To get us to that point our conversation moves through four themes.

The first is to understand anger itself. What it is and why it matters. In the first two dialogues we explore two distinct types of anger: tribal energy and moral outrage. We examine what constitutes a legitimate grievance versus an "identity regulator", and in doing so we uncover the underlying economic causes driving public anger. This provides us with a lens through which to make sense of the rise of populist politics. Populism is incoherent, but the energy of tribes and the moral mob are clearly identifiable. Those most angry are often motivated minorities – those most likely to vote – and street-smart intuitive politicians know how to exploit them. We should know when we're being duped and manipulated.

Once we know what we're dealing with, we want to understand "why?" and "why now?" To get there, in Dialogue 3, we try to give the best political economy story we can about how we got here. Political economy is where politics and economics come together to determine who gets what, where, when and why. To that end, Dialogue 3 gives a crash course in the long-run political and economic history of the world and explains why we periodically fall from economics into angrynomics. The bottom line is that we have been here before – angrynomics is recurrent – and large-scale macroeconomic crashes discrediting conventional models of thinking are its root cause.

If Dialogue 3 gives the bigger picture, the fourth dialogue discusses a distinct form of private anger – the anxiety and stress that can ruin our private lives. We identify the everyday or micro-level generators of angrynomics. We focus on two in particular: technology and aging. The first is super-hard to think about (because innovation and its effects are inherently unpredictable), and yet there are hundreds of books on how technology, especially artificial intelligence and robotics, is changing everything – even if it hasn't happened yet.

We hope to show that technology is changing some things, but not everything. And that a lot of what people say is really techno-babble and a bunch of fantasy-hawkers selling bits of the sky to each other and gullible investors. Entertaining, but not serious. We argue that just because a technology exists, it does not follow that it will be adopted. Technologists, especially those selling blockchain technology and cryptocurrencies, tend to forget that. What economists term the "rate of diffusion" – the length of time it takes us to absorb technology in our work practices and lives – is often far more important than the innovation itself. New technologies are rarely adopted overnight. They are constrained by institutions, social norms and costs, and they are always resisted and modified.

To investigate the second main source of our everyday anxiety, we focus on demography – the fact that the populations of the world's developed countries are getting older. Return for a moment to our synthetic economic world of representative agents, devoid of sex, age and ideology. Imagine if we populated that modeled world solely with old people? How would consumption change given that the old save more than the young and have already bought all that they need? What would happen to investment given that the old spend less? What would happen to policy given that old people vote twice as much as young people – almost everywhere? That's more like the world we live in. Aging has consequences for the economy that we hardly ever examine, but we really should, and those consequences create a lot of our stress.[7]

Dialogue 5 turns our own moral outrage to posit some creative solutions. A key point we want to make is that individual-level solutions to such problems simply don't work.

Like a libertarian who is rich enough to have his own fire brigade, it's really not going to help if the whole town is on fire. The solution to an angry world is not to individually insure against it, but to collectively embrace it. And that requires effective forms of collective insurance and distribution that are fundamentally different from the ones that we have in our minds, and in our politics, today. The good news is that the acceptance of a new set of innovative policies that takes politics beyond its traditional left and right boundaries is emerging.

Our proposals include the creation of national wealth funds to align the interests of business and labour, and to provide assets to those who have none. We propose an overhaul of how central banks work in order to provide new forms of social insurance and to shorten and reduce the likelihood of recessions. Zero or negative interest rates are often viewed as a cause for panic – far from it. Cooperation between fiscal and monetary authorities using a system of dual interest rates can supercharge the finance of alternative energy and regional development. We also propose a new fiscal rule, which is not just prudent, but consigns austerity to history, and provides ample scope to finance various forms of a "Green New Deal". We want to tackle wealth inequality without stifling genuine innovation. We want to encourage technological change and higher productivity, while securing decent, stable livelihoods for all in society. We demand that the planet thrive for our children.

Contrary to a great deal of populist pessimism, these objectives are complimentary and require neither new borders nor economic regression. One undeniable fact is that we have greater resources than at any other time in human history. We present radical proposals that disrupt traditional political divisions – they have advocates on both the left and the right

– which directly tackle legitimate sources of fear and insecurity, seek to restore the lost credibility of politics and restore the faith of populations in democratic governments. This is what makes us optimists. Our aim is not to make the world quieter or calmer just so that the rich can sleep sounder in their beds. Angrynomics is real and needs to be taken seriously. The point is not to quieten the anger because it's uncomfortable for those of us with the most comfort, but to listen to its legitimate expression, learn from it, and build a less angry world. This is how anger becomes opportunity.

Public anger and the energy of tribes

"Look at the anger, look at the fear"

NIGEL FARAGE

The parable of the angry folk singer

In the 1970s and 1980s, the British and Irish experienced local terrorism far more intense and frequent than anything the developed world has seen in the past 20 years. The Irish Republican Army (IRA) – a paramilitary organization seeking the unification of Ireland – declared themselves at war with the British state. The IRA killed 125 people in attacks in England, and over 1,500 people in Northern Ireland. Many more were wounded or maimed. Allegiance or opposition to the IRA split many families and neighbourhoods in the Catholic parts of Northern Ireland, and in some parts of the Republic.

Many years after the peace settlement and the IRA agreeing to disband, a denizen of Dublin went back there with a British colleague who loves Irish traditional music. So they went to a pub near St Stephen's Green, where traditional bands always played. In the pub there were maybe 30 or 40 people drinking pints of Guinness and listening intently. Ninety per cent were tourists

– Germans, Spaniards and Italians. Maybe more. There were also some lost-looking young women over on a bachelorette weekend, unconvinced by the fiddle, banjo and guitar players. Few locals were to be found in the audience. The band was great. They were playing both ballads and traditional dance music. But the lead singer looked pretty glum.

He had a great voice, but he was miserable. Inspired by a rather sombre number, he then launched, unexpectedly, into an intense political monologue. Although not angry, he was primed for it. Despite the past 20 years of peace, and an extraordinary economic boom in Ireland over that period, he began to talk about martyrs, hunger strikes, the oppressed Irish, and the fact that we "still have to free our country". And with his spirits lifted by nostalgia for the era of terrorism, he announced that "The next song I'm going to sing is a rebel song . . .". His references to past struggles – fictional and actual – against British rule were lost on his audience.

Peace had created a vacuum in this folk-singer's life. He was pining for that old era of tribal antagonism. Not for violence, but for the meaning that the conflict gave to him. It gave depth to his music. And it gave him a place to belong and feel valued. The only people who showed up that day to listen to his music and his republican speeches were foreigners. But that tribalism is back, and we need to understand the anger that drives it.

MARK: Okay Eric, the theme of this first dialogue is public anger and the energy of tribes. The idea that anger can regulate tribes is something people are unlikely to be familiar with. How does it help us to understand what's happening in politics today?

ERIC: Let's start with sports fans. Our propensity to seek group identity, and the motivation it provides, is deep-rooted. Even if all we have in common is the colour of a shirt, we will seek group allegiance, fight for our identity, regulate and threaten dissenters. The "angry fan" craves to be taken seriously, and that is significant. One of the first things I did when we started thinking about anger was a very simple big data analysis using IBM's Watson Analytics. I simply asked Watson to scan hundreds of thousands of news stories and sort those referencing "anger" into groups. The results confirmed public anger as an expression of moral outrage, but what really surprised me was the association with sports. Angry fans come up a lot.

Thinking about sports shows us how people enjoy tribalism – why else do we buy season tickets to watch teams that are rubbish? We pay money to be tribal. Sports fans also teach us that tribalism motivates: hard-core fans will travel to watch terrible games, in any weather, in locations that are difficult to get to. Once you are alert to the concept of an angry fan, *why* they are angry becomes clear. If you ever want to witness tribal anger, but can't face a political rally, go to a football match.

Interestingly, angry fans are nearly always a minority. Evolution has not made all fans angry fans for a reason. They are a functional minority. They are loyal, committed, potentially violent and feel the tribal identity strongly.

Also, when you study the tribal identity of sports fans, you realize that there is a hierarchy of loyalty and the angry fan is very high in that ranking. Often he (and as the literature on anger shows us, it typically is a "he") will regulate his own side. I have seen angry fans berating their own side for not chanting loudly enough, for not being committed enough. Their own players, managers and coaches are just as likely to be subjected to aggressive abuse – for insufficient commitment or for demonstrating a lack of group loyalty – at least as much as the opposing fans are. Indeed, some fans will even smash up large parts of their own city – and that's when they win (see Eagles fans' destruction of Philadelphia after Superbowl 2018). The angry fan regulates and reinforces tribal identity, which is an inherently political act.

Tribal identity and morality have one thing in common. Ethics and morality, the social codes that determine "the right thing to do", are primarily aimed at protecting our collective interests. Societies thrive because we have ethical norms of behaviour that support our common goals. Ethical norms solve what social scientists call "collective action" problems, which arise when there is a conflict between the interests of the individual and those of the group. For example, it is in everyone's interest to pay taxes, even though an individual would benefit if she doesn't. We typically solve this problem with independent arbiters, regulation and the threat of sanction, which is the main reason we have a judicial system, law enforcement, and indeed governments.

But when corporations or rich individuals evade paying taxes – like in Iceland – we get angry. Anger carries the threat of retribution when an ethical norm is violated. It's a way of saying, "stop doing that, or you'll regret it". The Icelanders reaction to the revelations of the "Panama Papers" was moral outrage. Their political elite appeared to believe that there was one rule for the many and another for them, the few. Violating that norm resulted in an anger that reshaped Icelandic politics. The ongoing unrest in France is motivated by the same emotion. We the people, in our common yellow jackets, against you, the cosmopolitan elites who tax us without representing us.

Now think about tribal identity more broadly. What is the social function of the tribe? It is very simple. Humans are much more successful operating in groups and being part of a group increases your odds of survival. But in a world of limited resources *you need to decide who is in the group and who is not*. We can't survive on our own, but we can't include everyone if resources are scarce. Our hardwiring to form groups is so profound that we will form tribes based on trivial differences – indeed, perhaps we *always* form them based on trivial differences.

In social psychology there is a very well established theory called the minimal group paradigm, which identifies that our predisposition to form groups can be based on completely superficial distinctions. In ancient Rome, for example, a chariot race that divided the city into different coloured teams produced riots that killed hundreds. Our propensity for group adherence is a universal, profound, and often imperceptible reflex. Little wonder then that it matters for our politics.

Now, not all groups should be seen as *tribal*. Tribal identity is a particularly deeply felt and existential form of group identity, which needs periodic enforcement and regulation in the same way that social norms do. Most of the time we are not focused on our tribal identity. We get on with our lives. In peaceful, prosperous times, tribal identity takes a back seat. But if we think we are threatened, if we think resources are becoming scarce, or if we are stressed – the minority of angry fans serves a function. They fire up the tribe for battle and keep everyone in line. Viewed through this lens, the parallels in contemporary global politics become clearer.

Current disputes over trade provide a good example. The great French anthropologist, Marcel Mauss, said "In order to trade, man must first lay down his spear". It is not a coincidence that Donald Trump has chosen trade as his antagonism of choice. It is also not a coincidence that the British right-wing, which is intellectually pro-trade, engages in absurd contortions and denials of evidence to justify leaving the most profitable free trading bloc in the world – the European Union – in order to set up new trade deals with other tribes deemed preferable.

MARK: That all makes sense. So we have two types of public anger. We have moral outrage – a legitimate response to being ignored, a vocalizing of wrong-doing, and a call for redress and action. That is the anger we should be listening to and responding to. On the other side we have anger as a tribal energy that can be cynically harnessed and weaponized by opportunists. But in viewing both of these forms of anger as emotions that function to solve a collective action problem – to help us survive collectively – you risk making tribal anger seem benign. Is it?

ERIC: We need to draw a clear distinction between legitimate public anger and the cynical manipulation of tribal anger for political ends. Indeed, I would go much further. By focusing on tribal anger I think we can make the case that an alignment of the interests of the media and the global political elite is using this energy to motivate voters and win elections, and this is extremely dangerous. Tribal anger is after all only one step removed from tribal violence. The challenge for a non-violent politics is to get the message loud and clear about legitimate grievance, and then to respond with an alternative politics. Why? Because any alternative politics has to matter – it must be significant enough on an emotional level to create political identities independent of tribalism. Tribalism is not the only motivating political identity, but it is a powerful reflex when we are stressed and angry.

22

MARK: Let's talk some more about this. Aren't political identities always tribal? I'm left – you're right, etc. Can we make a clear distinction between legitimate and tribal anger in our politics and economics, if everything is polarized and what's "legitimate" depends on which side of the fence you sit on?

ERIC: Party politics is often described as "tribal", but this is simplistic. Humans may be hardwired to form groups, but not all group identities are the same or equally motivating. Tribal identity, which has a tacit or explicit allusion to ethnicity, place or origin, is a very distinct way of aligning political orientation. Nationalism is the dominant modern form of political tribalism.

As our first parable alluded to earlier, I grew up with nationalism in Ireland. The constellation of political parties made little sense without reference to nationalism, because the Cold War legacy of a left-wing party on one side and a right-wing party on the other didn't, and still doesn't, really exist there. In Ireland, the party structure is a legacy of the 1922–23 civil war, which to a large extent reflected one's degree of allegiance to one faction of the Irish tribe. This still influences voting patterns today. What's instructive about the Irish example is that tribalism as a form of political motivation is powerful and enduring, and the political elite can and do use it to deflect us from their failings. Nationalism is a "political technology" that is everywhere used instrumentally by societal elites to secure their privileges. Whether it's Modi in India, Trump in America, Orban in Hungary, or Johnson in the UK.

Growing up with tribal politics made me very aware of its pernicious features. At one extreme there is a tendency towards non-democratic violence, manifest in the Irish case in a bloody terrorist campaign. But tribal politics is destructive in another way. It hijacks genuine political debate and deflects us from the issues that really matter to people, like wages, housing, health-care and education. Why worry about the influence of money in politics, or underinvestment in public services, when we can get vexed about Brexit and "the Wall" instead?[8] That way the elites are kept secure and we can avoid dealing with the hard stuff.

Tribalism, which was exploited by the political elite very early on in the Irish case, is now being mobilized everywhere. Consider the Brexit debate in the UK. Whatever ones' view on Brexit, EU membership was never the population's primary concern, and yet it has overwhelmed the government and it obsesses the political classes. It paralysed the UK for over three years. It deflects while it inflames. It disguises what's going on by blaming it on some other tribe. Tribalism today is being utilized by parts of the political class and a media under economic threat, to fill an identity-vacuum created by an anodyne and complacent political centre that has lost authority and the ability to motivate.

MARK: Explain why you think the political class is exploiting tribalism?

ERIC: I think there are two forces at work. First, politics has descended into the tactical mobilization of small minorities of the electorate in order to win elections. Close elections are decided by fractions of fractions. Second, there is a destructive symbiosis between the traditional media, which is under a rela-tively new but existential competitive threat from the internet, and the political classes of the developed world.

MARK: Please unpack those rather bold claims.

ERIC: It is a common mistake to think that democracy is majority rule. In the absence of a significant consensus, it rarely is. Majoritarian electoral systems are actually rule by minority, with protections, and the promise that "you get to try to win next time even if I win now". A truly fair electoral system may not be possible when there is significant disagreement. We accept the outcome of an unfair process because we can't think of a better way, and we collectively agree on the need for a peaceful transition of power.

We know from sports games that angry fans are a minority, and we know from research in political science that angry people are more likely to vote.[9] Harnessing tribal anger to motivate a minority can then be a winning strategy. Consider the United States where around 60 per cent of the electorate has a strong partisan allegiance. They are also more likely to vote than those without party allegiance. But winning a presidential election is primarily about motivating a significant minority that is not already committed, and we know from existing research that anger does just that. This becomes crystal clear in electoral tactics.

Trump won in 2016 thanks to 80,000 votes in three states. Motivating an angry minority won him the presidency. Trump instinctively exploited the two forms of public anger we identified. First, he appealed to legitimate moral grievance in the Rust Belt, citing the neglect of manufacturing industries, infrastructure, and Midwest communities by coastal elites, and then without missing a beat he shifted to tribal anger with images of walls to keep out marauding criminalized immigrants, in districts where racial tensions were elevated or nascent.

MARK: This is far less novel than it appears – there are direct parallels in Ronald Reagan's campaign strategies and Trump's.

In Reagan's case the tribal focus was in Southern states and the nod was to racial violence, which he picked up in turn from Richard Nixon. Likewise, Trump's "Tariff everyone" trade policy seems new, but people have forgotten the stealth trade war that Reagan fought in the 1980s against Japan, other Asian economies, and even the European car industry. We have been here before, but we forget that.

ERIC: In my view, beginning with the end of the Cold War, and accelerating through the crisis and crash of 2008, tribal anger has become a more pronounced and a much more global feature of political strategy. Much of what we are seeing is the cynical response by the political classes in developed countries to their loss of control over their economies and to the lack of a common political identity that they were unable to forge in the post-Cold War world. Tribalism is a motivating reflex to fill that vacuum, which is in turn amplified by a far more competitive mainstream media landscape and by social media.

The interaction between hysteria, stereotyping, fictitious enemies and fears, generated by the media, and among our online tribes, should not be underestimated.[10] Fake news has economic roots in the mainstream media. We don't talk enough about the incentives of politicians and the media, and how they align. Even in the case of Trump, who presents himself as at war with the media, there is a very clear symbiosis, and not just with Fox News. CNN would have less to talk about without Trump being in power. Similarly, no one really asks why the media developed an obsessive narrative around terrorism, Islam, and – in the UK at least – the stresses on public resources posed by immigration. I think a significant factor is that the mainstream media has faced its own existential economic threat over the same period that left-wing and right-wing identities failed. People like Trump give them constant copy.

MARK: This is an important point. Newspapers used to operate as semi-monopolies, with captive readerships. Yes, their proprietors had political goals, and they could influence and periodically determine elections. But they never had to fight for eyeballs. Even with the emergence of stable islands of readers built around paywalls, the shift in technology and the emergence of social media has brutally challenged these old media monopolies and confronted them with the reality of competition. *The Sun* newspaper in the UK used to sell over three million copies a day and determine elections. Now it's down to a million a day while Facebook matters much more. Given this, what better way to motivate a readership than with stories of fear, terror and foreigners over-running your lands? When we consider the set of forces at work, it becomes clear why tribal anger has become an exploitable resource of segments of the political class. Indeed, recent research shows how much even mainstream centrist politicians have adopted the language of populist outrage. It works to win. But when we think about the consequences and risk they are running with this it is paramount that we combat it.

ERIC: Electoral tactics and the economic insecurity of the media have coalesced to give rise to a re-emergence of tribal anger. But why now? Although the use of tribal identity has often been latent, tangential or local, why has it suddenly emerged as a global strategy?

MARK: I'd like to have a crack at answering that. I think this re-emergence of tribal identity is a much more long-run process than most people think. If we divide the post-1945 world into two eras: the Cold War world of 1945–89 and the subsequent era of so-called "neoliberalism" – the period when we decided to privatize, deregulate, liberalize and integrate anything that was once national and protected – what is curious about the Cold War-era is the extent to which fervent, motivating political identities were grounded in the economic ideologies of left and right, and these were in turn deeply embedded in social and political institutions, such as political parties, trade unions, working men's clubs, churches, and small business associations.

People in this period did not identify politically primarily based on tribal, ethnic and nationalist grounds, as they did in the Ireland that you grew up in. In most of the developed world, political identity during the Cold War years was grounded in what could legitimately be called an *economic ideology* – a collection of beliefs about the economy – concerning how it works, who owns what, who gets what, and why they do, or do not, deserve it. Whether you were pro-state, or pro-market, a clear set of beliefs about your economic interests, whether you were pro-business or pro-labour, was the name of the game. People also had a very clear sense of the real differences between political parties on fundamental issues of policy, and that their interests were being represented by one party and not the other. These ideologies motivated people to vote. Those identities were quite stable.

The post-Cold War shift to neoliberalism was not just a huge shift in economic organization, it also destroyed the political identities of a great many people, and not just the annoyed folk singer in our parable. Most people still trundled out to vote for "their" party after the Berlin Wall came down – Labour, the Social Democrats, the Democrats – but did it really matter anymore? The post-Cold War era was defined by a loss of political identity and the political disengagement of large parts of the population, especially by those most hurt by the economic changes of the period.[11]

In the Blair, Schroder, Clinton, Obama, centrist era there simply were no strongly motivating political identities or competing ideologies. Everyone was assumed to believe in some variant of a market economy and to embrace a cosmopolitan individualism. If you did not, you were considered a relic, or worse, a nationalist. When those ideas went up in smoke in the financial crisis of 2008, politicians had to find something new, and they did. So much of what we see today is politicians attempting to fill the vacuum created by a discredited neoliberal consensus with a more motivating set of political identities.

ERIC: So this rise in tribal anger, and its exploitation by the media and the political class, is not a consequence of the financial crisis alone, or even the sources of legitimate moral outrage such as the neglect of the US Midwest or environmental degradation. It significantly precedes these phenomena, and it exists even in economies that have been far less economically stressed. The hollowing out of democracy, the corruption of the political classes, the seeming irrelevance of elections, the inability to prevent recessions, increases in wealth and income inequality, and rapid technological change, all matter. But these stresses are channeled in different ways in different countries due to the coincidence of interests between politicians' need to motivate a minority to win elections and the legitimate grievances of those most affected. Modern tribalism has its origins in a loss of motivating political identity. The political classes have responded to the dilemma of how to get people out to vote in the absence of motivating ideas by reverting to tribalism.

I think the most instructive examples are to be found in central and eastern Europe. Why is it that the most successful cheerleaders of nationalist tribalism are to be found in places like Hungary and in Poland? These countries have two similar features, they were at the heart of the Cold-War victory of liberal, free-markets, and they are, relatively speaking, economic successes – they have had very strong real wage growth. Although Hungary was at the front line of the financial crisis in eastern Europe, Poland was one of the least affected countries in Europe. Since the crisis, both countries have seen big increases in living standards and a collapse in unemployment to historically low levels. But this has not hindered aggressive tribalism. Hungary's President Orban is very explicit about his strategy. He says that he abandoned liberalism to win elections. Being anti-European, anti-immigrant, and sectarian, wins elections in Hungary. The moral case for freedom and free-markets made by this once youthful anti-communist is a distant dream.

MARK: Okay, so let me summarize and set up where we are going next. When we analyze anger in our politics – especially public anger – it is important to keep tribal anger and moral outrage distinct. The financial crisis, the brutal recession in its wake, the euro crisis, rising income and wealth inequality, and an abject failure of political representation, are at the core of our problems. They are and should be objects of moral rebuke. But while these factors motivate anger, and that anger finds its way into politics, this has to be separated from the energy of tribes and the cynical exploitation by politicians and the media of latent nationalistic identities to get elected and to sell copy – how they chose to fill the vacuum created by an anodyne, identity-free, political centrism. The former we can and should do something about, and the policies we shall discuss later are designed to do just that. The latter we should expose and disarm since they are more harmful than the grievances that they are a response to. Okay, so let's turn to the lessons we can learn from *legitimate* anger?

The moral mobs and their handlers

"I am your voice"
DONALD TRUMP

The parable of the Spanish family who played by the rules

Pedro Garcia graduated in economics from the University of Cadiz in 1998. The Spanish economy was booming, and it didn't take him long to get a job working for a local bank in the mortgage approval department. Soon after graduating, he married his university girlfriend, Valeria. After a year of teacher-training, Valeria got her first job as a schoolteacher in a local school. In 2001, their first child, Anna Maria, was born.

Unsurprisingly, the Spanish housing market was much debated in Pedro's office. Young families like his were struggling to afford to buy properties like those of their parents. Prices had been booming for almost ten years. Some economists were saying there was a bubble. Pedro wasn't sure. He worried about the coastal property boom, but in towns and cities where he and Valeria wanted to live there would always be demand for good properties. Spain was in the European Union and had just joined the euro. Interest rates were lower than ever before, and the euro represented stability relative to Spain's past.

Pedro wanted to take out a big mortgage and buy a three-bedroom apartment in Cadiz, which they could just about afford. Valeria wasn't sure. Wouldn't it be wise to save more and perhaps wait for property prices to calm down? Pedro, and her parents, convinced her otherwise. "He has a good job in the bank, and you are a public employee, with high job security. Take out the mortgage and make a nice home for Anna Maria." They signed the deal in 2002.

Over the course of the next ten years, their plans fell apart. Pedro and Valeria saw the value of their house collapse. Initially, Pedro held on to his job, protected by Spanish labour laws, but his salary was cut. Despite working in the public sector, Valeria first saw her salary reduced by 30 per cent, and was then made redundant in another round of budget cuts.

Pedro and Valeria had never been interested in politics. They had open-minded attitudes about most things in life. They liked modern Spain and Europe. But Pedro also knew enough economics to know that you are not supposed to respond to a recession by making even more people unemployed in order to restore investor confidence – a policy called "austerity". When unemployment is high, high school economics says to cut taxes and increase spending. This "punishment" coming from the EU, was motivated by some perverse desire for retribution and was a dishonest attempt to deflect blame.

In reality, his bank, like all other banks, had miscalculated. They had assumed that property prices would always rise like they had in the past. He also knew that German banks had been encouraging banks like his to borrow from them and finance the property boom. The story being peddled by European politicians and central bankers of prudent Germans and spendthrift Spaniards was a lie. The German banks were bailed out by the European Central Bank, but it was public-sector workers in Spain, like his wife, who paid the price through budget cuts.

This wasn't the rational, liberal, open-minded European Union he believed in. This wasn't even capitalism as he had been taught it. It was socialism for the rich and bankruptcy for the poor.

Pedro was eventually fired after the rules protecting workers in the labour market were changed. His family could no longer meet their mortgage payments, and the bank repossessed their house. They moved in with Valeria's parents, and they never had the brother or sister they had planned for Anna Maria. The story of Pedro, Valeria and Anna Maria was repeated across Spain, Greece, Portugal and Italy. Is it any wonder Europeans are angry?

╬ ╬ ╬

MARK: In our first conversation, we described the role of tribes and the hijacking of tribal energy by the political classes. That is the pernicious and manipulative side of angrynomics. The parable of Pedro, in contrast, suggests claims of moral outrage and legitimate grievance. Pedro and his family did nothing wrong, their elites did, and yet they had to pay for it. If that is the anger that we need to listen to, what are we listening for?

ERIC: To tune in to that, we need to get a bit philosophical. Luckily, the American philosopher Martha Nussbaum has a brilliant book on the subject entitled *Anger and Forgiveness: Resentment, Generosity and Justice*. At the heart of her analysis is the identification of anger as a response to perceived wrong-doing. This is increasingly supported by empirical research, both in social psychology and neuroscience.[12] Alongside "angry fans" moral outrage emerged as the most significant correlate in the big data exercise I referred to earlier, which analyzed the many thousands of news stories relating to public expressions of anger.

Public expressions of moral outrage take a very specific form. Private anger is typically seen as a weakness, reflecting the fact that something is wrong within us. But public expressions of moral outrage are defended by justifying the anger itself. Typically, moral outrage appeals to *unfairness*, a *failure to listen* to those who are affected, and *a failure to recognize the interests of those most affected*. For example, expressions of anger against the imposition of austerity policies in Europe, as our parable highlights, follow this structure. The democratic process was frequently hijacked by technocrats enforcing "reforms" when there was no economic logic to support austerity.

Angry people who rejected this narrative were right to do so. Their anger is rational and legitimate. In contrast to tribal rage, people motivated by moral outrage can often very clearly articulate why they are angry – that their interests, or those they care about, are not being taken into account, and that the perpetrators of wrong-doing are not being sanctioned. This is very different to tribal rage, which seeks not justice, but to destroy anything in its way.

Nussbaum, very perceptively, identifies specific triggers for moral anger, such as "status-injury". She quotes the psychologist Carol Tavris' study of anger in America, and "finds ubiquitous reference to 'insults', 'slights', 'condescension', 'being treated as if I were of no account'".[13] I think this response resonates with our observation that anger is a demand to be heard, a demand for representation. But it is also an expression of intent and significance – *I matter and you better listen to me*. In the political context, this is very pertinent.

MARK: Given that, let's start with voice, because this is something that is central to understanding why people vote in ways that are often, patronizingly, described as "against their interests". People are not just angered by discredited and unjust policies. They're also quite-rightly upset because no one has listened to them, no one represents them, and because other people they perceive as part of this same elite are busy telling them what their interests "should" be.

We described the era of neoliberalism as fostering a loss of political identity – creating a vacuum that tribal anger has filled. But an unintended consequence of the post-Cold War political convergence between parties in the 1990s and 2000s was the emergence of a lifeless and largely self-serving technocratic centre, which caused large segments of the electorate to feel voiceless and unrepresented, which was steadily reflected in declining electoral turnouts.

Think back to Matteo Renzi, elected prime minister of Italy in 2014. This youthful new politician takes the reins of power and is ready to reform Italy, post-euro crisis. His first significant attempt at policy-making is to call a referendum on constitutional reform, which by most accounts seems like a sensible way to improve decision-making in the Italian legislature. But as Brexit showed us, if you offer people a referendum, and that's the only chance they have had to express their voice, they'll aim to be heard. And if it's Tweedledum and Tweedledee in every election – you can have whatever variety of economic neoliberalism you want, but it's always the same set of policies – then they will use that as a chance to vent their anger and frustration. The rejection of Renzi's referendum proposal was nothing to do with constitutional reform. Similarly, Brexit to many people had little to do with the European Union. This is really more about the demand to be heard.

ERIC: You might almost say that had there been an alternative ideology for people to express their frustration they would've done so – it just didn't exist. Indeed, if communism hadn't already been tried and shown to fail, the post-financial crisis period might have been its coming of age. Consequently, there has been nothing in successive elections that allowed people to express their discontent with the status quo. The option for non-nationalistic identity-based political change simply does not exist. Alternative visions to neoliberalism have not been offered by the established elite. So Brexit and voting for Trump becomes your chance to have a "f**k you! I want my voice heard" moment. From this perspective, public anger is a response to a lack of representation, to a real sense of being ignored and not listened to. It is also a failure to present a compelling and motivating alternative to the centrist consensus.

What has happened over the past ten years in Europe and America is similar. The political centre was totally blindsided by a crisis that they thought could never happen. And they had no response to it except to pile misery on the very people who didn't cause it. Unsurprisingly, those people got very angry about that, and that anger has been amplified and hijacked in multiple ways.

From the American Midwest to the North of England, from Italy and Spain to Greece and Portugal, all these countries have experienced serious economic trauma over the past decade, and the political classes not only offered no alternative, but told their citizens that it was their fault: "You borrowed for a house you could not afford", "There has been an orgy of spending that we need to stop", etc. So when there was a chance to vote for an alternative vision, as for example in Greece in 2015, or in the UK in 2016, or Germany in 2018, it should come as no surprise that that is what happens.

But this story has deeper roots than the 2008 crisis and its economic legacy. Specifically, a lack of voice is related to the sense that the nation state has been neutered by globalization. At some level, it is not just that the population at large feel unheard, and the empirical research shows that they are not listened to, but that their traditional representatives also seem resigned to their situation: "Globalization made us do it", "There is no alternative", etc. This certainly seems to be a major concern, and the rise of nationalist politicians seems to be the result. The lack of voice paired with a perception of futility is a toxic mix. It's like voting for populists in Italy and then figuring out that they can't do very much either. The result undermines democracy itself.

MARK: As I try to think about it, you have markets, whose reach is global, or at least as far as the division of labour, technology and finance allows them to go, and then you have democracy, which is inherently local, bound by this thing called the nation state and the people, the citizens, that constitute it. This generates an inherent tension between the openness of the global economy and the responsiveness of the state to the democratic wishes of the public. The more open you are, the less control you have. The less control you have, the less you can respond to what the global economy demands that you do. The economist Dani Rodrik usefully calls this the "political trilemma" of the global economy, where globalization, democracy and sovereignty are mutually incompatible in such a way that you can only ever have two out of the three.[14] And once you have accepted globalization, you can either have democracy or sovereignty, but not both.

To preview what we will discuss in the next dialogue, we have been through two big iterations of this tussle between

states and markets, between openness and democratic responsiveness, in modern times. The first set of rules was established in the aftermath of the Second World War and the Great
Depression. The new rules were about limiting the reach of the
market through controls on finance – making sure that capital
is invested at home – targeting full employment to prevent the
1930s returning, and imposing high taxes and transfers across
the economy in order to build a welfare state.

This system, as we shall see, functioned quite well for about
25 years. But the flaw was that it generated inflation, and
labour's bargaining power eroded profits causing declining
investment spending. The response to the stagflation of the
1970s – falling growth and rising inflation – was to "disin-
flate" by opening-up financial markets, privatizing state assets,
deregulating businesses, thereby "freeing" capital from the
constraints of the nation state to find its highest return. This
was construction of what we call today the neoliberal order
– what Rodrik calls "hyper-globalization".

If you were an investor in the years after the Second World
War, you were bound to the territorial nation state, which
meant that local labour could quite effectively exercise its voice
through strikes to claim its share of productivity gains. But
what happens if capital can go global? What happens if capital
can exit the nation state but labour stays local? Or if they can
move your job abroad, which is the same thing really? They
take away the ability of labour to demand their share, along
with their voice. And since the 1980s this is what has increasingly happened.

Labour's ability to demand their share of national income
declined dramatically, and business entered a new golden age
– as did inequality. The numbers are now so well-known as to
be commonplace. According to the World Income and Wealth

Database – the source with the most complete picture at a global level – the top one per cent globally captured as much income growth as the bottom 50 per cent of the entire world economy since the end of the 1980s. Across Europe the top 10 per cent have 37 per cent of national income. In the US the figure is 47 per cent, which is higher than in Russia. In the US in particular the rise of the one per cent has been accompanied by the collapse in the income share of the bottom 50 per cent from 22 per cent to 13 per cent of national income. The poor really have gotten poorer as the rich have gotten richer.

In the UK after the crisis real (inflation adjusted) government spending fell by 16 per cent per person. At the local level it fell by nearly a quarter, with some areas losing nearly half, yes half, of their budgets.[15]

You will not be shocked to know that the areas with the deepest cuts swung most heavily nationalist (to UKIP) at the time of the Brexit referendum.

Given this, when we talk about the rise of tribal political parties emerging under angrynomics, we need to stress that this is absolutely not about reigniting a latent tribal political identity that is somehow genetically inherited. England, after all, has only been around in its modern form for a few hundred years. And yet here is a genuine sense in which much of the political class, everywhere, at a national level, feels both neutered and powerless in the face of globalization while nonetheless profiting from this skewing of incomes. Regardless of whether it's left-wing or right-wing nationalism, the re-emergence of so-called "populism" then becomes phrased as the struggle to protect the nation and the national economy against "outside" forces that produce these inequalities. The Brexit campaign slogan of "Take back control" resonates for a reason.

I think we can also see this very clearly in the 2016 US

presidential election. It is very telling that the five states that were supposedly solidly blue-collar Democrat, but turned out for Trump, were the ones that suffered the most in terms of de-industrialization and the export of jobs. One of those states, Wisconsin, lost one third of its industry, not to Mexico or China, but to Southern "right to work" (union-free) states in the 1970s and 1980s as business migrated south. Wisconsin has been in relative decline for a very long time. NAFTA in 1994 and then China joining the WTO in 2001 accelerated that feeling of decline and actual job losses, and over time the Democratic Party coalition that tried to embrace unions, free-up trade, and profit from global finance all at once fractured. After all, these policies of trade openness and global capital were championed by Democratic administrations, but mainly hurt Democratic Party loyalists.

These dynamics, and not just in Wisconsin, have been 30 years in the making. As I noted earlier, back in the 1970s, we had a world where labour unions were strong and because capital was local rather than global, they had real bargaining power against capital if they went on strike. In such a world workers could get a better deal in terms of how profits were shared, and we saw this in the data. Labour's share of national income in the US peaked in 1973 and has been in decline ever since. That decline parallels the rise of a world where unions are all but extinct in the US and are much weaker than they were in Europe. Even German unions know that globalization starts 60 km outside of Berlin with the threat to move jobs to Poland should German workers ask for more than whatever their employers are willing to give.

Similarly, in politics, parliaments are increasingly impotent with the important stuff given out to technocrats – to independent central banks, to the WTO, to the EU. The elected politicians are effectively governing over less and less at the same time as the stresses on their constituents, macro and micro, are increasing. We went from a world that was very labour friendly, relatively closed, and that provided a social safety net, to a set of institutions that generates a massive skew in the returns going to the very top of the income distribution while uncertainty for the majority increases – all while the media tells them that it's their fault.

ERIC: Okay, so the first clear source of legitimate anger is a loss of voice – anger as a response to being ignored, or having your voice taken away from you via an empty "democratic" ritual. Representative politics, through the emergence of a post-Cold War technocratic centrist consensus, stopped listening. This was compounded by globalization – particularly the free movement of capital and the inability of labour to negotiate its share – and in Europe, by the power grab of a centrist technocracy.

You argue that these concerns pre-date the financial crisis and need to be seen in the context of 30 years of political and economic change dating back to the 1980s. At the same time, something manifestly went wrong in 2008, which you describe as "super-charging" these latent trends. The parable of the Garcia family, which started this dialogue, gave us a sense of this. Voice matters most if we have something important to say. Why did our political and economic elites have so little to say in response to the 2008 financial crisis?

MARK: For me, the primary problem was *who* they listened to rather than what they had to say, and it wasn't the Garcia families of this world who caught their ears. Rather, the failure of policy-makers to deal effectively with the recession following the 2008 financial crisis, and subsequently the 2010–15 euro crisis suggests that like income, listening skews to the very top. The euro crisis, much more than the crisis in the US, showed beyond any doubt that a policy of cutting spending in a recession only ever makes things worse. But they knew that already and went ahead and did it anyway. And then they doubled down on it, even when they saw it wasn't working.

The severe recession that began in 2009 triggered legitimate anger. In the United States, joblessness rose to the highest level of any postwar recession, and the recovery was tortuously slow. Recessions of this severity and duration impose terrible economic and social costs on the public. In Europe matters were even worse. Despite being the supposed home of ample welfare states, which have in reality been dying a death by a thousand cuts for the past 20 years in many cases, we haven't seen economic devastation of this order of magnitude since the Great Depression. Greece instigated more spending cuts than any country and unsurprisingly they lost 25 per cent of GDP and a third of all jobs in doing so.

ERIC: The most extreme case is Greece, but Portugal, Spain, and to a lesser extent Italy, saw similar economic and social damage. Much of southern Europe has experienced persistent youth unemployment rates of 30 or more per cent for almost ten years. Yet, this is completely unnecessary and is the result of grotesque policy errors. If we know one thing in macroeconomics, it is that mass unemployment is a terrible blight on society with long-term consequences, but it can be eliminated relatively quickly with two simple policies of demand management: by governments cutting taxes and spending more money, and by central banks printing money.

But those countries in the eurozone who have no currency of

their own can neither devalue their currencies to grow through exports, nor can they inflate their way out of trouble by bailing out their banks directly. As such, their elites appeared to have neither the vocabulary, nor the means politically, to meaningfully address these policy errors. After all, having signed up to the euro project, they can hardly then disavow it.

Given this, the Italian, Spanish and Greek political systems can offer nothing to their populations to convincingly address their concerns, even now, when the immediate crisis is over. It is abundantly clear that the Italian unemployment problem is cyclical. It has nothing to do with changing the laws in Italy. It has to do with aggregate demand management in the eurozone. The same is true of Spain and Greece, and if you accept this, there is a major problem.

In such a world the domestic political process becomes seen as a sham. You can have an election, but you can't change anything. The local political elites may know this – and they may not even like it – but when you don't have your own currency and central bank, what can they do? You can neither devalue nor inflate nor default, so you have to cut your way to prosperity, which doesn't work. It is entirely logical under such conditions that electorates will get angry and seek alternative solutions. Indeed, you don't even have to be in the eurozone to end up in the same situation. Look at British politics and the Remain campaign's fear-mongering message "there is no alternative" after several years of similarly destructive policies.

Tribalists, in such a world, will happily supply alternatives, no matter how high the bullshit content of their offerings. This is exactly what we saw in the 2018 election in Italy, which resulted in a bizarre allegiance between neo-fascist northern separatists, and a party founded by a putatively leftish comedian, with most of its support in the South.

The US case seems different and yet the anger and the polarization in US politics seems, if anything, deeper still. Despite claims that the US is not really divided, and that most people actually agree on most issues when polled, organized politics is still fiercely divisive.

How do we explain this, given that the economic landscape in America is so different to that of Europe? It can always be argued that the US fiscal and monetary authorities should and could have done more, but it remains the case that America under Obama embarked on one of the largest fiscal programmes of the postwar era, and it is very hard to argue that the Federal Reserve under-reacted. The recovery was painfully slow, but the US has still enjoyed one of the longest uninterrupted periods of jobs growth on record. This is not some depression where people who want work can't find it. The opposite is true.

There is a legitimate question about the quality of the jobs being created, and data from the Federal Reserve on Americans' subjective assessment of their economic well-being shows how this recovery slowly recovered jobs, but not wealth. Approximately 74 per cent of American adults in 2017 said they were either doing okay or living comfortably. And at the same time, 40 per cent of American adults said that they would not be able to cover an unexpected expense of $400.[16] A later 2019 Federal Reserve study showed us why. Despite being ten years after the crisis 60 per cent of Americans have not rebuilt the wealth that they lost in the crisis.[17] So despite a putative recovery, discontent persisted due to the precariousness by which many Americans live and the thin or non-existent wealth cushion they rely upon in moments of stress.

MARK: I do think that the micro-stressors causing angry-nomics, which we will explore in more detail in Dialogue 4, differ significantly between the US and Europe. We think of Europe – in part because we hear this in the media all the time – as being in need of "structural reform", which until recently has largely meant pushing down wages in order to raise national "competitiveness". But unfortunately doing that destroys demand because if you cut everyone's wages to be more competitive there is simply less demand in the economy and between economies, which ends up actually harming employment. There's not that much wrong in Europe, structurally. That may be a surprise to some people, but when you consider that northern Italy has one-third the poverty rate of the United States, why is it that we hear that Italy, rather than the United States, needs the reform? Europe has a lot going for it, it's just got the wrong policy mix in terms of one currency, one central bank, one interest-rate, all imposed on this hetero-geneous group of economies.

The United States is an interesting contrast insofar as while it now has full employment, the benefits to growth are far from evenly spread and the recovery, as you note, has not really been a recovery except in terms of the employment rate. Or take healthcare as another stressor. In the United States you really have to worry about healthcare, it's a personal consumption expenditure. Your employer, if you're lucky to have one that still does this, pays for a bit of it, and you pay for a bit of it, and increasingly the employers have been paying less and less of it. In that type of labour market, you've got much more sensitivity among workers to their real wages than in, for example, Italy where you can get by on €1,200 a month, because healthcare is not something you have to worry about as an impoverishing out-of-pocket expense. You simply cannot get by in metropolitan areas in the United States on $1,200 a month without falling into poverty. So although there are common global themes behind the public reaction to perceived economic injustice, there are very different micro-stressors at work in different geographies.

ERIC: Okay, so when we look to the causes of legitimate public anger, we have a series of factors emerging. At the root of this is a perceived and genuine loss of political power at the level of the nation state. That loss of voice is grounded in two structural trends: globalization, which undermines the genuine power of the nation state in certain important areas of policy-making, and a transfer of significant power to independent institutions, such as central banks, away from the elected political classes. At the same time there was the loss of the strong political identities created during the Cold War. The anodyne centrism on offer gave aggrieved voters little sense of either representation or choice.

The 2008 financial and economic crises brought these underlying tensions to the fore. Rule by technocracy lost credibility in the face of an economic crash, taking a particularly pernicious form in Europe, where the serious, grey-suited bureaucrats became a vehicle for meting out economic punishment, causing high unemployment and social deprivation, primarily across southern Europe. In the US, the crisis marked a discrediting of financialization and deregulation, reinforcing a sense that not only are economic gains concentrated in the hands of very few, but that government only acts to bailout the powerful and influential, while the consequences of recession are borne by those on low- and middle-incomes.

What remains striking is that throughout this we have an abject failure of policy. Rather than presenting a major programme of economic reform, the global political elite has offered nothing substantive, instead choosing to either jump on the bandwagon of nationalism or insist that nothing fundamental is wrong. Current political trends are, in part, a confused reassertion of the nation state to mitigate the consequences of unconstrained capital flows and the power of business more generally. But the deep economic sources of legitimate public anger remain unaddressed – our failure to deal quickly and powerfully with recessions despite knowing how to do so, and the major surge in inequality in income and wealth that has happened across the developed world as capital prospered and labour stagnated.

We will return to our proposals to fundamentally tackle the risk of recession, but I think it is worth us spending some more time on inequality, as the picture may be less straightforward than is often presented. Despite the fact that many of the features of the trends in income and wealth inequality date back to the early 1980s, the topic has only started to dominate political discourse across the developed world in the last five to ten years in particular, highlighted by the publication and extraordinary success of Thomas Piketty's *Capital in the Twenty-First Century*.

Also, it is a very complex area – measurement is extremely difficult, and there is a lot of difference in the trends geographically. I want to stress one of the sources for my caution about the role of inequality as a *singular* cause behind angrynomics is that anger is a universal feature of politics across the world, but trends in inequality are not. Inequality is a problem for many reasons ranging from creating different life-opportunities for different classes of citizens to creating different health outcomes. All of these are well-known and documented. But I want to stress something else that we have hinted at so far – how uncertainty creates more serious stressors in the lives of individuals who find themselves at the wrong end of the income distribution. I would argue that that this uncertainty – over income, job security, over your future prospects and those of your children – combines to create a sustained private anxiety that also feeds angrynomics.

MARK: We have multiple causes of inequality. No doubt. We know that policy has contributed to this directly through product and labour market deregulation, the de-unionization of labour markets, and through tax policies that favour the top earners. It is also well-recognized that technology has contributed to both greater income and wealth inequality. We have also talked about the tension between nation-state level political decision-making and the power of global capital, which has also affected the distribution of national income between labour and capital. But I want to explore in some more detail your caution around the role of inequality in the generation of public anger. Why do you want to pull back on making the rise in inequality our "prime suspect?"

ERIC: My first observation is the empirical fact that the trends of angrynomics seem uniform across the developed western world, but the picture on income and wealth inequality varies considerably. But there is a deeper point relating to measured material progress and a sense of well-being. I think people conflate two issues when they talk about inequality – claims that median real incomes haven't grown over the past 30 years, which is primarily a US phenomenon and which may have reversed, and an observation that the dispersion of wealth and income has increased. I am of the view that inequality has risen to unacceptable levels, but I am very sceptical that median real incomes haven't grown, and that matters.

MARK: Okay, explain to me why incomes have grown more than we think?

ERIC: One defence of the market system and the inequalities that it generates is that it raises the standard of living of the overwhelming majority of the population, including those at the lower end of the income distribution. For that reason, in a sense, we collectively tolerate much of the inequality. So it matters if real median wages and incomes haven't grown. If they have not, the system is failing.

Stagnant real wages imply very little improvement in standards of living, so we need to be sure that is indeed the case, and I am not. Indeed, I am also sceptical of arguments that the neoliberal era delivered no real income growth for the lowest deciles of the income distribution, even in the United States, because our measures of real incomes are very imperfect, and the constituents of these cohorts are not stable.

Here's one problem. When people talk about the real median income not growing since the 1970s, the measurement of inflation is a critical component of that. We know what nominal incomes have done. That is, money wages not adjusted for inflation. But we don't know what prices have done, and measuring prices is a surprisingly hard thing to do. For example, if inflation has been over-measured by 1 per cent for 20 or 30 years, real incomes could be 30 or 40 per cent higher than that implied by the data. A more prosaic example is that if Walmart keeps cutting prices, the real wage of their customers has gone up even when their pay is stagnant. It may not feel like a pay increase, but it is one, because what really matters is how much consumption your wages can buy.

The evidence that we do have on this suggests that inflation is indeed over-estimated by around 1 per cent per annum due to a number of technical challenges in the way inflation is calculated, but primarily due to changes in the quality of goods and services – think of going to the doctor today compared to in 1978 – which are very difficult to measure. It is almost certainly the case that this measurement problem is more acute in a service-based economy with rapidly changing technology than for the manufacturing one we had 40 years ago. And most of what we consume today are services, not goods.

MARK: First of all, I have a problem with this line of argument because if you don't know how big the error is you can't know to what extent it matters. It might matter, it might not matter. Moreover, if inflation has been mis-measured, then it's been mis-measured for everyone. The poor may not be as poor as we think, but the rich must also be richer than we thought such that the inequality itself may not be altered. But more importantly, how does that story fit in with the standard sets of numbers that we know from the work of economists like Piketty, Milanovic, Saez, and everybody else? That the 1 per cent have made off with 90 per cent of the income gained since 2012 and that they went from around 8 per cent of national wealth at the end of the 1970s to almost 28 per cent of national wealth today?

ERIC: My argument doesn't change the fact that inequality has grown and is extreme. I think this is a major problem. But my point is that it is likely that the neoliberal economic order has actually delivered economic gains to all. It has not been as zero-sum as is often portrayed, and I suspect that the measurement issue is a significant factor here. I also think that there is an important difference between the distribution of consumption and the distribution of income. In Europe, an unequal distribution of income is less important because the services we care most about, such as healthcare, are provided for free. In America, the cost of healthcare, and often education, is astronomical.

I should also emphasis – and this is very important – that it is perfectly possible that the global liberal economic system delivered economic gains for the overwhelming majority of the population, to varying degrees, but simultaneously people still feel profound anxiety and distress. I think this comes to the fore when we look at the micro-stressors of angrynomics. I think it is very plausible that technology has raised real incomes and made us unhappy. Smart phones being a case in point.

MARK: But could this measurement issue bias things the other way, such that inequality in consumption is worse than we think? For example, measured inflation in the US has hovered around 2 per cent for the past 20 years. Over the same period education costs have gone up 120 per cent and healthcare has gone up 80 per cent. Apparel goods have fallen in real terms, so I guess we can all look good while being super-stressed and angry as hell while not being able to go to the doctor. The quality of care may have gone up. But access is down, so who cares? Similarly in Europe, the services that are free have been subject to rounds of cuts even in the most prosperous countries while demand for them has skyrocketed. That foodbanks are free and plentiful is not something to be celebrated.

ERIC: Again, the US is very different to the rest of the developed world. Cancer is one of the biggest sources of personal bankruptcy in the United States. In most of Europe, cancer treatment is free and is, on average, just as effective. Healthcare costs may be *understated* in the US data, precisely because many people in America can't actually afford it. Furthermore, the fear and stress over getting ill in the US exists, even if you don't get ill. These are all fair points.

MARK: Okay, I get all that. But it complicates much of what you said before about anger. If the righteous anger that you want to listen to is misguided because people can't figure out the difference between real and nominal incomes, we don't know what we are listening for. After all, if people are richer than they think, we are back to square one in terms of explaining how the economy generates angrynomics. So here, perhaps, is a different way of framing the problem that addresses your objections in part.

When you look at much of the academic literature on populism it tends to fall into three genres. The first could be called "it's all culture". This genre likes to focus on Trump voters and tends to ignore that there has been a left-wing as well as a right-wing populist reaction in and beyond the United States. Nonetheless, there is certainly something to it. Perceptions of status-loss among working-class male populations, reactions to the elite embrace of multiculturalism, the deaths of despair from opioid and alcohol addiction documented by the economists Anne Case and Angus Deaton, and simple racism, are clearly present.[18] But such factors characterize what's there, they don't explain it. The problem is that you can't explain a cultural change by reference to a cultural change. For example, explaining a rise in racism by a rise in the number of racists, or vice versa. That's both circular and true by definition. Something has to be causing that rise in racism apart from the thing itself or the thing it's measured by.

This brings us to the second genre, which we can label "it's all economics". Now, being angry economists we like this one more. But if we are fair, we have to admit that it is also partial. It downplays the cultural and perhaps tries to explain too much through correlations. For example, the Brexit vote correlates with budget cuts and import competition, without explaining why these material changes are producing the anger that populist politicians are exploiting, and why now? After all, we have had recessions before, but they have seldom led to political ruptures on this scale.

The third genre defies a quick description, but essentially it stresses two causes: geography and skills. Cities are the winners and the skill-shift towards educated white-collar workers drives a lot of the inequality we see. Smaller cities and towns away from metropoles are the losers. What goes along with that is the second set of causes: the blindness of the elites in these cities to the travails of the rest of their fellow citizens. Christophe Guilluy's *Twilight of the Elites*, beautifully tells this story for France, but more recent work shows that this urban/rural, skilled/unskilled split is significant everywhere. The French "Yellow Jackets" protest seems to back this up.

Now, rather than pick and choose, what would allow us to unite all three approaches? To me, it's inequality. If people perceive nominal to be real and real to be unreal, then what matters is what they think and not our measures of what they should think. Inequality is as much perception as it is material, just as what is seen to be a "fair" distribution matters as much as an equal one for driving anger.

What drives white working-class status anxiety? A new and sudden desire to be racist? Or the fact that they feel that someone, somewhere, in some big city has made off with all the cash, while they get less and less, all the while self-interested politicians tell them it's all gone to minorities and foreigners?

What drives people dependent on the state to vote against the EU when the EU has nothing to do with the inequity of the cuts that they feel? What makes the Yellow Jackets take out half the traffic cameras in France other than a feeling that they are being fleeced for driving to work while the elites in cities take more and more? Regardless of how it's measured, it's the perception and fact of inequality that, for me, drives angrynomics. I think if we accept that we can explain an awful lot of what's going on.

ERIC: I buy that – up to a point. At a very fundamental level, our feelings around status and justice, the semi-ethical drivers of anger, are ultimately about perceptions of relative treatment and access to resources. But I would still argue that the thesis around angrynomics that we are presenting is more nuanced and revealing about our true challenges and anxieties than the simple material inequality narrative permits. You can experience an increase in income and feel greater insecurity and stress. Inequality may be a proxy for something deeper. Ironically, I am predisposed to the view that tackling inequality is part of the solution, but the role of inequality is exaggerated as cause.

Now before we wrap up this dialogue on moral outrage as a form of public anger, can you succinctly present your thoughts on an important area we have so far neglected – demography? We will talk more about it in Dialogue 4, but just give an outline now. In our mind's eye we often think of angry old men, but when we think of football fans it is angry young men that spring to mind. Always men it has to be said, but anger doesn't appear to be the preserve of any age group. How does demography feed into angrynomics?

MARK: Yes, this is one part of the puzzle which we are going to explore in more detail in our fourth dialogue. Consider the following. In general, across the rich countries of the world, income within the 50–60 age group can range as widely as it does between a 20 year-old and a 40 year-old. Now that's a fact. But this is also a fact. Pretty much all rich people are old. They have had a lifetime to accrue assets and they acquired them in a particular historical moment of high real interest rates.

In the immediate postwar world these inter-generational transfers were less of a problem. There was a large public sector that transferred income between age cohorts and generations. People, and corporations, paid higher taxes. Pensions were relatively low shares of total public expenditures. Today, with an increasingly aged population, and after picking up most of the wealth generated in the past 40 years along the way, you have a situation where pensioners have lower levels of poverty than the young, are more likely to vote, have claims on a huge part of the national treasury because there's more of them, and they're living longer. Their consumption is also very different. They save more and spend less, which lowers growth for everyone else. Once you add those aspects to our story, you see a picture of inequality across generations, as well as between classes and between the owners of different assets. Add an aging population to technological innovation in an angry and uncertain world and you get, once again, a toxic mix that is fueling our politics perhaps more than we think. We'll return to this later.

ERIC: Okay, so that brings our discussion of public anger as moral outrage to a close. We have identified a series of forces that coalesced to undermine our sense of voice. The financial crisis and its aftermath brought this and other underlying economic tensions to the fore. The effects of recession and a secular trend in inequality provide legitimate economic reasons for anger. The regional picture is nuanced. We have argued that income inequality may matter less in Europe because income itself is less unequally distributed, but also because critical components of consumption, healthcare and education, are either a lot cheaper or provided for free, even if their supply has been constricted in recent years.

The problem in Europe seems to be an inbuilt tendency towards financial and cyclical instability that is causing a severe and structural problem of unemployment, and in many countries, relative wage stagnation. In the US, the problem is reversed. Healthcare costs, in particular, are debilitatingly high by global standards, and income inequality is more extreme. We can argue about the long-term trend of real median incomes in America, but the reality is that the vast majority of gains have gone to the very top of the distribution, while a simple illness can bankrupt an American family. Demography, as we shall discuss, is exacerbating trends that have been caused by policies of deregulation, a shift in the balance of global power towards capital, and the well-known destabilizing effects of technology.

Our bottom line is this: no one has imagined, let alone implemented, a politics and a set of policies capable of tackling these issues. We believe there are some smart ways to do just that and in doing so provide an antidote to angrynomics. But to get there, let's now figure out in more detail how the hell we ended up in this mess in the first place. A world that has never been wealthier but seems so angry.

Macroangrynomics: capitalism as hardware, with crashes and resets

"We praise a man who feels anger on the right
grounds and against the right people"

ARISTOTLE

The parable of the three economists

Karl was, if truth be told, more of a historian than an economist. Indeed, deep down inside, he thought that the whole turn of the world in the nineteenth century to market exchange, wage labour, and making everything into a commodity for sale for the sake of profit, was a thoroughly bad idea. His hunch was that labour was unique among commodities in that it was not really a commodity at all. Labour was, after all, like Soylent Green, made of people. And while Soylent Green cares not a jot what it costs, people do. And if the world around them changes in such a way as to make them poorer, through no fault of their own, they will get very angry and demand that the state protect them against these "market forces". People laughed at Karl. They assured him that markets were as natural as the air we breathe, and provided, as Dr Pangloss promised, "the best of all possible worlds". And then the world collapsed in the 1930s and people everywhere rebelled against markets.

John was, if truth be told, more a mathematician and a philosopher than an economist, but perhaps that's why he could discern another truth. That supply does not create its own demand because individuals' decisions to consume and save and invest are separate from each other in time. Once you realize this, recessions and depressions suddenly make sense. If investors get depressed about the future, they will not invest now, which brings about the very outcome they are trying to avoid in the future, a recession. John thought he had found the answer to curing depressions. It's simple really. If your expectations of the future are depressed, all you had to do was spend some cash today to raise the level of prices tomorrow, and investors would start investing again today, anticipating profits ahead. The point of spending was not spending. It was to shift expectations of future profits. But when John's ideas became popular, Mikhał, who came from the same part of the world as Karl, found a flaw in John's logic that echoed Karl's hunch about labour.

If John's solution was to raise prices to prevent recessions, Mikhał figured out that doing so would result in a shift in power from business to labour. Specifically, if full employment were guaranteed, labour could move costlessly from job to job, all the while bidding up the wage they received in permanently tight labour markets. This would cause business's profits to fall, labour's share of national income to grow, and diminish the political clout of the investor class.

Mikhał mused that the inevitable result would be a revolt by capital against labour and a reinstatement of market discipline. After all, if Karl was right and labour, facing wage cuts, would turn against markets and turn to the state for protection, all business needed to do was take over the state and roll back those protections to restore their place at the top of the table. So, the project became to reverse Karl's protectionist impulse, which is oddly, exactly what happened in the 1970s and 1980s. What then is the point of this parable? It tells us that at the end of the day you may have the perfect technical answer to an economic question, but if the politics are against you, you're done.

֍ ֍ ֍

ERIC: Mark, we have outlined two forms of public anger. One form – the most pernicious and virulent – is the energy of tribes. It has been exploited by segments of the political classes and the media to motivate a minority that is angry and tribal. It polarizes, and it threatens violence and discrimination. Angry minorities can and do win close elections. The second form of public anger, which we need to listen to and address, is moral outrage. People have been neglected, ignored, disparaged, and the political classes have failed to listen to their genuine concerns – job insecurity, a loss of skills, rapid changes in working practices, a loss of representation, wealth inequality more extreme than anything we've seen since the roaring twenties, political corruption, and a discredited elite. This is political anger as a form of legitimate moral rebuke. It has economic origins. But it has a history and a backstory. Let's try and piece together that story as best we can.

MARK: Okay, let's use an analogy we've used before when trying to get people's heads around the long-run story of angrynomics. It's an analogy of capitalism being like a computer that crashes from time to time. This provides a simple model for thinking about the macro-story behind angrynomics. Let's walk through three · versions of this capitalism/computer analogy that we can call versions 1.0, 2.0 and 3.0. Now, with that as a preamble, let's get started.

ERIC: Before discussing each of the versions, let me talk about the hardware of capitalism. Imagine your tablet or laptop is a capitalist economy. That is, an economy where the production of goods and services is provided by individuals and firms through markets where who gets what is rationed by prices and incomes. If you dropped the laptop on the floor and picked up the pieces, you will find the hardware that makes it work. If your laptop or tablet is an Apple product, it will be configured (the bits fit together) in a certain way. That configuration will differ from, say, a PC laptop, or a Samsung tablet. They each have essentially the same components, but the "plumbing" of how they fit together is different.

Now go back to a real economy we live and work in. Just as every computer has a motherboard, a memory, a video processor, and a central processor, so every capitalist economy has a labour market, a capital market, a government, and a host of other similar component parts. And just as Apple and Samsung products are configured differently, so is the arrangement of the components that make up real economies.

Imagine, for comparison, the US and German economies. The US labour market is lightly regulated, produces large numbers of workers with general skills, training is done by institutions external to the labour market itself, such as colleges and universities. In contrast, in Germany, the labour market is much more regulated, it produces both more highly skilled workers, and many of those skills are produced by training within labour market institutions such as trade unions and firms.

Now think about stock markets. The US stock market is huge, deep, liquid, and the goal of many companies is to get listed on the market and for the founders to cash out as quickly as possible. The hardware of the German economy is dominated by a network of typically small and medium-sized, often family-run businesses. Typically, they never bother to list or issue shares. The same contrast exists between the US and German governments. They are both federal states, but one taxes and redistributes large portions of national income and the other one does not, comparatively speaking.

The take home on all of this is that like computer hardware, the way that capitalist institutions quite literally fit together limits the type of policies that can be produced. If you have deep, liquid, and open equity markets, you can get most of your population to buy into equity based private pensions. If you don't, you can't. If you have large trade unions that control skills development, you don't move production to Mexico or China quite as quickly since you will not be able (easily) to find the skills you need. Okay, so that's the hardware, but what about the software – that is, the ideas we have about how economies can and should work that gives us the "code" for running the hardware?

MARK: Just as the configuration of the hardware limits what outcomes the machine can produce, so it also limits the type of ideas – the software – that can be run on the machine. For example, given German institutions, it would be next to impossible to run radical libertarian software on the German economy. Likewise, given US institutions, running the software for, say, Swedish social democracy, is likely to raise severe incompatibility issues. Just as software and hardware must be aligned on a laptop or tablet – you can't run Apple's operating system on a Samsung tablet without a lot of editing of the software – so they must be aligned if capitalist economies are to function. Moreover, given that different hardware and software configurations have emerged over time in different places, it should not be a surprise that what Denmark produces, consumes and values, should be different from what China produces, consumes and values.

Now, with all that in our heads we can map how different economies – different combinations of software and hardware – have emerged over time, and how they periodically produce a lot of anger. The key here is recognizing how "bugs" arise in the software that eventually crash the machine. When that happens, just like a computer, capitalism "crashes" and needs a system reset. The hardware needs to be reconfigured and the software needs to be rewritten, and sometimes it is, and it's usually a painful process. These crashes are the periods that generate lots of anger. To see why, let's go back to our opening parable.

The Karl in our opening parable is not Karl Marx, as you may have thought. Rather it was Karl Polanyi, a historian and sociologist. Polanyi wrote a book in 1944 called *The Great Transformation* that captured the essence of the bug in the software that killed version 1.0 of liberal capitalism, the version that emerged in the nineteenth century, spanned the globe by the turn of that century, and crashed and burned in the aftermath of the First World War. To find that bug, Polanyi asked the following question.

Markets, trading, and prices have existed for as long as humans have been around, so what is it that makes economic organization "capitalist"? Polanyi argued that what made capitalism distinct from previous modes of economic organization was that it rested upon the deliberate construction by the state of three "fictitious" commodities: labour, land and capital, without which you can have markets and exchange, but you can't have capitalism.

The most important fiction, as the parable explains, is that labour is a commodity. That is, a sack of potatoes, or a ton of wheat (or Soylent Green) is manifestly a commodity and doesn't care what it costs. But labour surely does. It likes when its price (wages) goes up and hates it when it goes down. When you continually push wages down – under a deflationary Gold Standard in the 1920s or under the "countries must be 'more competitive' with each other" dogma in the eurozone in the past decade – you end up creating a great deal of uncertainty and hardship for the people involved. People hate that stuff and get angry about it. Labour is the only commodity capable of generating a social reaction to movements in its price, which is why the notion that labour is a commodity like any other is a fiction – or at least a well-maintained political and legal construct – necessary for capitalism to function.

Polanyi's insight boils down to this simple point; the more that you try to treat wages as a price, as just another cost to minimize, the greater the social reaction against market exchange it provokes. If the version of capitalism you happen to inhabit has very few safety nets, and market relationships are the only ones that you can access to survive, there will be a demand by the citizenry for protection from the ups and downs of the market itself. Polanyi called this the "double movement". That is, any attempt to create a society dependent upon markets that treats labour like a commodity will inevitably produce a backlash against those policies precisely because labour is not a commodity like any other. That backlash will take the form of demands for "protection" from the market.

That protection in turn can take the form of trade unions, it can take the form of Joseph Chamberlain's social imperialism, it can take the form of New Deal liberalism, or Italian and German fascism. Today, it takes the form of an economic nationalism that, in the words of Brexiteers, seeks to "take back control" and make the economy more responsive to politics. In short, if you want to understand what happened in the 1920s and 1930s when capitalism version 1.0 crashed, it's really a story about the attempt to sustain the economic fiction of labour as a commodity coming up against a political reality, which is that if you treat people like a sack of potatoes they end up throwing *the system* into the fryer.

ERIC: Now, if Polanyi gives us the first piece of the puzzle regarding where today's angrynomics comes from – from the fiction that labour is just another commodity, which is politically unsustainable in practice – then the second piece of the puzzle comes from our friend John in our opening parable. John is, of course, John Maynard Keynes, who wrote a book in 1936 that was also a reflection on the failure of Capitalism v.1.0 called *The General Theory of Employment, Interest and Money*.

Prior to Keynes, economists thought that left on their own markets clear (buyers find sellers and workers find employment), and through free competition full employment would be produced. Keynes argued against this view, drawing on his understanding of the then on-going Great Depression, arguing that most of the time we don't actually inhabit a world where markets always clear and the poorest improve along with the richest. Instead, the world produced by capitalism can be one of high unemployment – or even a full-blown depression – and great inequality. There is no natural tendency for the system to attain the best of all possible worlds.

Given this, Keynes comes back to the role of the state as does Polanyi, but from a different angle. Keynes wants the state not just to act as a law-setting institution that creates Polanyi's fictions that makes markets possible. He wants the state to counteract emotional swings in private sector spending that cause depressions, by using public expenditure to stabilize employment and investment.

Now what does all that mean in the real world, and how does it relate to Polanyi? It means that in the period from 1870 to 1930, during Capitalism v.1.0, states could allow millions of workers to become unemployed and say "this is the natural order of things" because there was no alternative software (ideas) to run on the existing hardware (institutions). Indeed, the main safety valve of the period was immigration from countries with excess labour to countries with too little labour, hence Ellis Island and the rise of the United States.

But at its core, the software running on v.1.0 said that any attempt by states to do anything about "bad" market outcomes – such as unemployment or poverty – would be counterproductive as the market would in the long-run sort itself out. But when the multi-faceted cataclysm that was the 1930s occurred – the effects of pent-up First World War inflation on savings, the failed attempt to restore the Gold Standard, the Wall Street Crash, the collapse of global trade – all of which compounded the pressures on labour, v.1.0 collapsed. As Keynes famously said, it turns out that "in the long run we are all dead", and the death of v.1.0 produced three distinct expressions of public anger.

The first one was fascism. Fascism was an attempt by the state to save the market by abolishing society. It is "totalitarian" in that the fascist solution to anger is for everyone to be disciplined by the state so that tribal anger is displaced onto the "foreign" and the "impure". The second one was communism, which is an attempt to use the state to abolish the market, thereby disciplining society through class homogenization and the forced elimination of inequality to produce model subjects.

The last one is the most adaptive, a combination of democracy and markets, because in a democracy you get to vote, which gives legitimate voice to anger. But the problem with giving a voice to anger is that in v.1.0 what matters is money, not voice, while what matters in a democracy is votes. These two currents rather obviously come into tension. Capitalism version 2.0, if it was to survive, had to resolve that tension by making democracy and markets work together rather than undermine each other.

MARK: This bring us nicely to the content of Keynes' 1936 book, which was the new software written to make democracy and markets work together in Capitalism v.2.0 – the system that ran from 1945 to 1975. To clarify how different these two software programmes were, consider the two simplest ways we could write down the software for version 1.0 and then the software for 2.0. The software for v.1.0 is often called the quantity theory of money, but here we will take it as the basic software rule for running capitalism v.1.0.

$$MV = PQ$$

M = money;
V = its velocity (how rapidly it's spent in the economy);
P = prices;
Q = quantity (all the stuff in the economy).

So (M)oney times its (V)elocity of circulation must equal (Q)uantity (all the stuff in the economy) and the (P)rices denominate them. Easy.

What we have here is a very simple model of the world where on the left-hand side we have the monetary side of the economy (Money times its Velocity – how fast it's spent, basically) equal to the real side of the economy (the quantity of all the stuff produced (Q) times the prices we pay for it (P)). Now, here's the trick. MV = PQ is a truism. It's true by definition. But if I assume that over the long run (or in the absence of state interference, market imperfections, and/or Martian invasions) that velocity (V) is stable, I can make some powerful claims, for example, that if you increase M faster than Q it will show up in an increase in P (inflation) and if M drops precipitously then P will do the same (deflation).

In this model, Q, which is the total of economic output generated in free markets by capital and labour, should be left to its own devices. The state should limit itself to carefully controlling M, which generates inflation. So, there is a definite politics here. In v.1.0, (M)oney is kept in an anti-democratic box, away from meddlers and popular demands, and in return the owners of capital and the investor class – those at the helm of the growth machine – give us ever-rising standards of living.

Given the way this software was meant to run, the Great Depression came as quite a shock since it seemed that the only explanation for the mass unemployment of the period was that millions of people randomly went on unpaid leave, for years, and the desire to invest left the investor class. Clearly this software rule was bust. But what was the alternative? This is Keynes' alternative software rule:

$$Y = C + I + G + (X - M)$$

In this world money disappears, and the state comes back in.

Y = total income of everyone in an economy;
C = total Consumption;
I = total Investment;
G = government expenditure;
(X − M) = net exports; placed in brackets because in the context of the 1930s and the postwar 1940s the economy was largely insulated from outside forces.

Keynes' trick was to admit fully that (I) investment was the most important part of the equation and to agree with the v.1.0 view that without investment (I) there can be no wage growth, no productivity increases, nothing. But, he argued, what happens in a depression is that investors' expectations of future profits get crushed (who opens a new factory in the middle of a recession?) and once those expectations get embedded among investors as a class, it becomes irrational to invest. G − the government − has to spend money, not to pay-off clients or bribe the voters, but to alter the price signals to which investors respond, making it rational for them to invest again. This is why government spending is central to Keynes' view of the world. But once again, there is a politics to this, a politics that Keynes himself denied, and that is what effectively became the bug that crashes v.2.0.

If, in the first equation, it's the individual capitalist and investor who is the hero, investing and bringing things to the market (Q), then in the software for v.2.0 it is government spending (G), which drives and regulates the level of private sector investment (I). In v.2.0 it is government spending, not the animal spirits of the private sector, that is the key to stabilizing demand and ending recessions. Given this, if you want to avoid fascism, communism, and put markets and democracy together productively, government spending to maintain consumption to avoid recessions and depressions is critical. It's a feature, not a bug. Successfully targeting spending by running budget deficits when needed becomes the key software rule, with full employment, high wages, constant productivity improvements, and a high level of redistribution through taxes becoming possible in v.2.0 for the first time.

This was the software that produced the postwar welfare state and the postwar growth story. The desire to permanently quell the anger that the crash of v.1.0 created drove the development of new software and a full hardware reconfiguration to boot. With the very real fact of communism in Berlin in 1945 focusing the minds of policy elites in the West, and the combination of depression and war breaking the old hardware, the advent of this new software for running the machine created the room for a massive reboot of the system.

That reboot was hugely successful. For the first time, right across developed countries, the top of the income distribution in every country came down, the bottom went up, and the whole distribution moved up together, for nearly 30 years. This was the period when French national income tripled, the Italians talked about "Il Boom", the Americans discovered the middle class and British Conservative politicians built millions of units of public housing and boasted that the working class "had never had it so good." Indeed, they had not.

ERIC: It's important to stress how different the new system was. Regardless of national hardware variations and local software modifications, one policy target – full employment – was the common goal of all nations. This had never happened before.

But since the 1920s and 1930s had shown that unemployment and poverty made people angry to the point that the system will collapse, the new system reset was designed to make sure that didn't happen again. But to sustain full employment and high real wages, the hardware of v.2.0 had to be fundamentally rebuilt too.

First, finance had to be put in a box and locked away. Finance that built factories and invested in technology was fine. Finance that sought to short currencies and speculate on bonds was banned. Banks were kept in restrictive silos that limited what they could do – in the US and the UK – or they were legally mandated to be heavily capitalized thereby limiting their leverage – in continental Europe.

Labour was legally recognized as *not being a commodity just like any other*, and collective bargaining between unions and employers became the norm. This gave both sides political leverage, which meant that productivity gains were (more) evenly split between capital and labour. This, in turn, meant that if capital wanted to increase profits and full employment was the target, they would have to increase productivity to do so, which stimulated further investment. This produced a virtuous circle where high productivity created high wages, which meant high consumption and high tax revenues, all of which enabled the production of high quality public goods (healthcare, education, housing) that lowered labour's dependence on the market still further and took the anger out of the system.[19]

And all of this was buttressed by a set of international monetary institutions and agreements that kept exchange rates stable and capital local.[20] This was a radical and deep-seated hardware reconfiguration and software reboot that enabled countries as different as the United States and Sweden to sustain full employment as the policy target for three decades, until the wheels, rather unexpectedly, fell off the wagon. Because just as there was a bug in the software of v.1.0 – treating labour as a commodity while denying the possibility of involuntary unemployment – so there was a bug in this system too. Which brings us to Michał, the third economist in our opening parable. You know all about this guy, Mark, so over to you.

MARK: In 1943, in the midst of the war, and with the revolution in economic ideas about full employment in full swing, the Polish economist Michał Kalecki wrote seven pages of text for the journal *Political Quarterly* that not only identified the bug in the software of v.2.0, but predicted what v.3.0 – the world we grew up in – would look like. It's an amazing piece to read, even today.

Kalecki argued that Keynes missed the politics of sustaining full employment over the long run. Far from being welcomed by the investor class, sustained full employment would consistently push-up wages and kill the returns to investment. Put simply, if the labour market is consistently tight, then the dumbest people in your firm can leave work at noon and get a new job at a higher wage by 4 pm. While this would clearly benefit labour, it would lead to capital thinking that this new state-led labour-friendly version of capitalism was, at the end of the day, a really bad deal.

First, given strong labour unions and costless mobility from job to job, management's "right to manage" would be undermined, and labour indiscipline, especially strikes, would spike. This is exactly what happened in the 1970s across the rich countries of the world. Second, the only way that firms could hold onto skilled workers given such pressures would be to pay them even more in wages. But the only way that firms could absorb those costs would be to raise prices ahead of productivity. But if all firms respond this way it ignites a wages-chasing-prices-chasing-wages spiral of inflation that in turn provokes more strikes as workers realize that the wage increase they just secured is eaten away by inflation. It would also be the end of high wages forcing firms to be more productive. This is also exactly what happened in the 1970s.

Crucially, an unanticipated acceleration of inflation acts as a tax on the returns to investment that, as Keynes realized, retards future investment. Basically, if I am an investor and I expect to make a return of 5 per cent real over five years (net of inflation) on an investment in an environment of 3 per cent inflation, I need to make an 8 per cent return. But if inflation unexpectedly accelerates over that five-year period, to say 10 per cent, and my costs rise in line with inflation, my returns are destroyed. Given this, Kalecki predicted that under a policy of sustained full employment investment would fall and inflation would continue to rise, even as labour markets were tight. Once again, he was exactly correct.

Think about this for a moment. Kalecki had predicted in 1943 "stagflation" – the simultaneous combination of unemployment and inflation in the 1970s. The inevitability of a system of closed economies driving consumption and targeting full employment had to produce an inflationary crisis for investors. This was the bug buried deep within the software of Capitalism v.2.0.

Kalecki even predicted the beginnings of the reboot to v.3.0 that started in the late 1970s and which was completed two decades later. He said, and it's worth quoting him here, that because of this crisis of profitability, a powerful block is likely to be formed between big business and the rentier [financial] interests, and they would probably find more than one economist to declare that the situation was manifestly unsound. The pressure of all these forces, and in particular of big business, would most probably induce the Government to return to the orthodox policy of cutting down the budget deficit.

(Kalecki 1943: 330)

Yes, he had just predicted Margaret Thatcher, Ronald Reagan, the liberation of finance, and the beginnings of Capitalism v.3.0.

ERIC: So, if the problem with Capitalism v.2.0 was a wage-price spiral damaging investment and ultimately scoring an own-goal against the objective of full employment, then v.3.0 was specifically designed to restore the power of capital, deregulate markets, and destroy inflation. Now, it's actually quite easy to kill inflation if you are willing to deal with the political fallout. You simply push up interest rates, as Fed Chairman Paul Volcker did in 1980 by rationing bank reserves. Doing so makes borrowing and debt expensive, and as a result businesses fail, demand falls, unemployment rises, and a deep recession squeezes labour and pushes inflation down, which is what both Reagan and Thatcher did in the early 1980s. But to keep it down and ride that political storm you needed to fundamentally change the software and reconfigure the hardware once again. The new software that was written for v.3.0 was the revolution that had taken place in macroeconomic theory during this disruptive period. Tell us about that.

MARK: These are the ideas that we were raised on in our classes at university in the 1980s and 1990s. The lesson learned was that the software running Capitalism v.2.0 could not generate stable inflation and low unemployment at the same time. This, plus a turn in economics to more microeconomic approaches provided the political representatives of capital – Kalecki's "Powerful Block" – with their new software. We call this set of ideas "neoliberalism".

But to run this new software you had to do more than simply tweak the old hardware. You had to fundamentally reconfigure it once again. The new policy target for v.3.0 was not full employment – for that produced inflation – but "price stability" – that is, guarding against inflation at all costs. Although raising interest rates will crush inflation in the short term, to make this permanent hardware changes were needed that would destroy the ability of the system to generate inflation in the first place. There were four key hardware changes that took place in the 1980s, which took inflation out of the system permanently, restored the value of capital, and in doing so built the world that we grew up in.

The first was to destroy the power of organized labour to raise wages. Whether it was done through outright confrontations with organized labour epitomized by Thatcher's bitter battle with the British National Union of Miners in the 1980s, or through the migration of business to "right to work" (union-free) states in the US in the 1970s, or through EU-level policies for greater "flexibility" in the 1990s, union membership everywhere plummeted, and along with it so did labour's ability to capture the gains from productivity increases. This in turn shows up in how much income labour takes home from GDP growth. It has fallen dramatically. Given this, the ability of wages to rise ahead of productivity falls drastically.

But what really accelerates these trends are two other hardware reconfigurations: the opening-up of financial markets and the globalization of production. A key hardware modification of v.2.0 was the insulation of the economy from financial flows. Basically, if you wanted to increase investment at home, you had to stop it going abroad. That meant banks were restricted in what they could do, as we've already noted. But in lifting those restrictions, a process that began in the late 1970s and was completed, more or less, by the late 1980s, capital was free to find its highest return, wherever that may be. Add to this the technological changes that made the globalization of production possible, such as the invention of the container ship, the IT revolution, and the rise of multi-platform production and offshoring, and labour's ability to demand real wage gains is further disabled.

ERIC: Version 3.0 was then predicated on allowing capital to be free to find its highest return. But doing so has costs. Huge flows of capital, and rapid reversals, caused a series of increasingly severe booms and busts across the developing world, culminating in the Asian and Russian crisis in 1997–98. The developed world proved similarly vulnerable during the euro crisis. Northern savings flooded southern markets after the creation of the euro in 1999, looking for higher returns. As post-crisis fears over the stability of southern European banks and governments built, these flows reversed, exacerbating the pain.

MARK: Correct. One of the main arguments for v.3.0 was that capital would be more efficiently allocated, and at one level it was. But what that means in real terms is that investment leaves capital-rich countries and ends up in capital-poor countries,

ANGRYNOMICS

such as China. Western firms benefit from this, as do their shareholders. Consumers in western countries benefit from cheaper goods, but the investment that would have happened in their country now happens elsewhere, which is a cost. This is why trade is now such a contentious issue.

ERIC: Finally, locking this in was the biggest hardware modification of all in Capitalism v.3.0 – the rise of so-called "independent" central banks. Remember that quantity theory equation where the state controls M and raising M caused inflation? Logically then, once you have disabled labour's ability to generate inflation, the only other possible source of inflation is the state since that prints the money (M). And with the rise of global financial markets that can punish states for policies that they don't like by taking their money out of the country, devaluing the currency, and causing a crisis, the case for giving authority over monetary policy to an "independent" agency, which took the long view rather than allowing politicians that always took the short-term view to make policy, became compelling.

And so, over the course of the 1990s, this hardware modification spread across almost all the machines running the software for v.3.0 as central bank independence, and the rise of the central banker as the most powerful policy-maker in the land, spread across the OECD and beyond.[21] The result was a system that was once again similar across those countries that produced common outputs, but those outputs were the complete opposite of v.2.0. Comparing versions 2.0 and 3.0 in a table can clarify this.

Capitalism v.2.0 1945–80	Capitalism v.3.0 1980–
Policy target: Full employment	*Policy target:* Price stability (low inflation)
Policy outcomes: Labour's share of GDP at historic highs	*Policy outcomes:* Capital's share of GDP at historic highs
Corporate profits low or stagnant	Wages low or stagnant
Inequality low	Inequality high
Markets mostly national	Markets globalized
Trade unions strong	Trade unions weak
Finance weak and immobile	Finance strong and highly mobile
Central banks weak and politicized	Central banks strong and independent
Legislatures strong	Legislatures weak

MARK: But as you stressed in the previous dialogue, Eric, one of the reasons v.3.0 lasted as long, if not longer, than v.2.0, was the fact that it worked. It restored the value of capital and crushed inflation. But in doing so, it set the system up for not one, but three bugs that would crash the system in 2008.

The first bug was inequality in income and wealth. One of the signature claims for the boosters of v.3.0, as it was for v.1.0, was that while the new system was geared towards capital rather than labour, the resulting growth would "raise all boats", or at least "trickle down" to everyone else. However, the problem we discovered by about 1995, through the work of economists such as Tony Atkinson, Martin Wolf, Thomas Piketty and Branko Milanovic, was that it was all trickling up, not down.

The numbers are well known, and we have mentioned some already, but just to recap, remember the following.

While globalization certainly benefitted workers in the developing world, workers in the bottom 50 per cent of the global income distribution captured only 12 per cent of total growth. Meanwhile, the top one per cent of the global income distribution made off with 27 per cent of total growth. While some countries have held the line more than others, almost every country has become more unequal over time, especially in countries such as the US that had relatively high income inequality to start with.

But inequality is only a bug if another bug shows up, which it did in due course. That bug is wage stagnation, which is what happens when labour's ability to take their share of growth is politically hamstrung by a combination of globalization, technological change and the assault on unions. Now I know you have some qualms about this regarding the measurement of inflation, but the key point is relative. If wages are rising for the bottom 60 per cent of a country's workers, then it matters much less that the top 10 per cent or above are making even more. Growth, like poverty, is relative. But v.3.0 not only generated inequality, it generated relative wage stagnation for the majority of workers in the developed world, and in some cases real income losses, especially in the last ten years of the regime.

Again, for illustration, according to many accounts, using US data, the bottom 60 per cent of US workers have not had a real wage increase (money wages less inflation) since 1979. And while measurement of inflation and other factors complicate this picture, as you said earlier Eric, what is indisputable is that dispersal across the wage distribution has increased too. Here's a fact that illustrates that brutally. Wall Street bonuses in 2015, when the economy was still healing from the crash of 2008, totaled $28.5 billion. That's twice the total wages paid to every person in a minimum wage job in the US that year, which is around 3 million workers.

In sum, Capitalism v.3.0 had three bugs. The first bug was trickle-up inequality. The second was wage stagnation and massive dispersal across the wage distribution. The third was a response to both of these factors that ended up compounding them – one of which you are most familiar with: leverage in the banking system. Why don't you talk about that?

ERIC: Okay, I will. Banks are funny things, even at the level of language. What the bank thinks of as an asset, we think of as a liability – a car loan, a mortgage, a student loan. A bank has no interest in owning your house, it wants the income stream that the loan to buy the house generates. So assets and liabilities together sum to zero. Similarly, one person's interest payment is another person's income, and that sums to zero too. This is why economists sort of forgot about finance being a problem. If it all sums to zero, who cares?

Why we should have cared is nicely illustrated by Citibank's 2003–05 advertising campaign, which ran billboards across America with the tagline "Open a Cravings Account – Live Richly".[22]

If my wages are not growing and all the wealth the economy generates is going to capital, and not labour, how can one "live richly?" The clue is that Citibank is a bank, and your liabilities are their assets. In short, you borrow. Massively.

When Fed Chairman Volcker increased interest rates in the early 1980s at the same time that finance was being liberalized it ushered in a period where real interest rates (the nominal rate minus inflation) stayed high while inflation fell fast. The

result was that finance suddenly became fantastically profitable and finance makes its profits by providing credit.

So, if you expect Capitalism v.3.0 to keep you in your job and maintain your standard of living you can borrow more against your future income. And even if your wages are not rising, with interest rates gradually falling, as they did by the 1990s from the very high real rates of the 1980s, you can still keep borrowing more. And borrow we did, with US and EU consumer credit almost doubling relative to disposable income from the 1980s to the mid-2000s. But if interest rates are falling and the banks make their money through loans, how can they still make money?

The answer is simple: make even more loans, with the end result that the system as a whole becomes very highly

leveraged. And in pursuit of ever higher profits banks themselves borrowed more to lend more, with the result that banks'
equity fell to only a fraction of their assets (mainly mortgages),
often by a factor of 30 to 1. Given this, when a bunch of mortgage companies and mortgage bond funds started failing in
2007, it didn't take long for it to develop into a full-blown crisis.
The losses in these markets ate through the banks' relatively
small equity base, rendering them insolvent. The system as a
whole had a heart attack called the "credit-crunch".

In short, Capitalism v.3.0's combination of rising inequality
and stagnant wages could be made to work so long as inflation was low (yes), interest rates were initially high but fell
over time, encouraging further borrowing (yes), and the ability
to borrow was unlimited. When the system crashed in 2008,
it exposed just how much leverage there was in the banks. It
exposed how polarized in terms of income and wealth countries had become, and how this whole system rested on
finance constantly churning loans from one part of society to
another and from one country, as in the case of the eurozone,
to another. And it all rested, once again, on Polanyi's critical
fiction, that labour was a commodity just like any other, and
that people don't get angry when they figure out they are being
treated as a commodity. Unfortunately, it seems that they do.

MARK: In fairness, given a shock of this magnitude, and given
how interconnected and leveraged the global system of banks
had become, the politicians in charge of Capitalism v.3.0 had
a tough choice to make. Version 1.0 crashed in the 1920s and
staggered on until the 1930s, when it finally fell apart, with
disastrous results. Version 2.0's crash provoked a lot of anger
too, but the reboot was thorough, and it seemed stable until
the inflationary bug began to play havoc. The problem with

v.3.0's crash was that the world had become so financially inter-dependent and "globalized" that it was feared that the system as a whole might go down like in the 1930s. So rather than allow it to fail, we turned to the central bankers, the new guardians of the system, and told them to bail the whole thing out.

Central bankers are a bit misunderstood. Even if they are independent, they ultimately take their orders from governments. And when a global banking system reliant on borrowing and lending in dollars blew up, the US Federal Reserve stepped in and gave almost any bank, anywhere, who needed it, access to US dollars to keep them afloat, almost regardless of country of origin. Eventually, the Fed, the Bank of England, the Bank of Japan, even the European Central Bank (eventually) bailed out the system, to the tune of around $17 trillion. And while such action saved the system, it was too late to avoid a global recession, the near bankrupting of Europe, and as a result of a series of major policy errors, unemployment in parts of Europe reaching levels and for durations not seen since the 1930s. Also, after the initial panic had been contained, it led to the tightening of government budgets around the world – so-called austerity policies – which made matters worse.

But what also mattered in producing angrynomics this time around was that it was ordinary taxpayers who were paying the brunt of these costs through unemployment, reduced consumption, bankruptcy, and through the micro-stressors that these generated from drug-fueled deaths of despair to increasing suicides, taxpayers who in many instances were already heavily indebted and had seen their own incomes stagnate for years.[23] They saw some of the richest members of their societies being bailed out as they were flung out of work. Labour was once again a commodity. Capital was protected – epitomized by the US insurance company, AIG, paying out hundreds of millions in bonuses in 2009 after being bailed out by the taxpayer to the tune of $180 billion.

The bottom 80 per cent were effectively paying for the mistakes of the top one per cent, while in the process bailing out the assets and incomes of the top 20 per cent – right across the world. It was, as I described it at the time, "the greatest bait-and-switch in human history" as the private sector liabilities of the banking system ended up being put on the public balance sheet of states as more public debt, which was then blamed by the political classes that had allowed all this to happen on a crisis of "overspending" by states that simply didn't happen in the first place.

Not many people know the intricacies of the banking sector, but they do know when they are being ripped off. Whether it was the Tea Party movement in the US, outraged at capitalism for the people and socialism for the banks, Los Indignatios in Spain protesting austerity cuts, or in the UK with Brexit, the crisis provoked a politics of anger that is now transforming politics everywhere.

And if we think in terms of the three bugs that together brought down v.3.0 – wage stagnation, bank leverage and inequality – we can see that these bugs in the system still remain. Despite a return to full employment in many economies, wage growth has been relatively weak for the majority of workers. The banking sectors of the developed countries are now more concentrated (have even fewer players) and are as profitable, if not more so, than a decade ago. Meanwhile, inequality remains stark. All of which continues to produce a huge amount of tension in the system, what systems engineers call "constrained volatility", that increases over time. And that volatility constraint has to blow up at some point.

ERIC: So why hasn't the system crashed again? Some of the bugs in the software have been fixed. The banking system, on most standard measures of risk, is much, much stronger. Also, policymakers were completely terrified by the financial crisis, which makes them highly alert to repeating the same mistakes. These factors alone may explain the extremely stable rate of global growth. But there's still a problem, I feel. And it's to do with moral anger.

The injustices writ large by the crisis, and the reassessment of 30 years of deregulation cannot be assuaged by continuing with the status quo. Capitalism v.3.0 got bailed out without a reset. The consequences of neither rebooting the system, nor doing anything to remove the bugs in its software has produced another deep bout of anger. That anger is bubbling up slowly, building momentum, and it is systemic, deep rooted, and it is here to stay.

Populism is the result of not resetting the system after a crash. Whether it's the anger that gives us polarization in US politics, populism in German politics, or Brexit in British politics, the system should have been reset and it wasn't. By failing to make fundamental changes to a system that has become a stress generator for the majority of those populations, we have created the conditions for another round of transformative angrynomics.

We should not be surprised by this. As we have discussed in this dialogue, macro-systemic crashes always produce public anger. That anger can be righteous indignation that can be addressed, or a tribal energy that can be weaponized. We are in the midst of one such moment. But that is only the half of it. The other half is the micro side of angrynomics.

Microangrynomics: private stressors, uncertainty and risk

"Whatever is begun in anger, ends in shame"
BENJAMIN FRANKLIN

The woman out of time

Francesca Salvo is a 78-year old retired academic who lives in London. Her parents migrated to London from Italy in the 1950s. Her father worked as a waiter and his mother as a cleaner. They eventually saved enough money to open an Italian restaurant in north London. Francesca was the brightest of three children. She excelled in mathematics and graduated in computer science from Imperial College in the early 1970s. She married a fellow academic, an English man. When Evan died from lung cancer at the age of 50, Francesca never quite recovered. She never met anyone else. Her two children, and her work, became the focus of her life.

Francesca officially retired 15 years ago but continued to carry out research and teach some courses for postgraduate students. With so much more free time, she decided to buy an apartment in Florence, near where she was born and had spent the first nine years of her life. She was still in touch with cousins and relatives. She loved going back to Florence. She had a passion for art and red wine. Her children would often visit, and she took them on tours of the Uffizi gallery and to see the frescos at the chiesa di Ognissanti. When they had children of their own, she still encouraged them to join her in Florence. There was just about enough room. She took her grandchildren for walks in the Boboli gardens.

As Francesca became older she struggled more and more with her trips to Florence. Instead of going once every couple of months, she went only two or maybe three time a year. Travelling was very tiring. The queues seemed longer at the airport. Maybe it was immigration. Too many people. She couldn't understand why security was so complicated. She would forget to take out her perfume, although sometimes it got through unnoticed. Her son kept telling her to travel light, but she didn't understand. You can't just put everything on your phone. She needed medicines for blood pressure, for cholesterol, and for diabetes. She had been told to take a double dose of vitamin D and vitamin C for her immune system. And she could never find the right ones in Italy.

She also found it increasingly frustrating the way that Florence kept changing. She bought her milk and eggs, fresh pesto and cheese in the *pizzicheria* around the corner from her apartment. One year she returned, and it had closed. The elderly owners had retired. The little *pasticceria* closed too. Noisy bars and even more little restaurants seemed to be opening everywhere. And there were lots of Romanians and other eastern Europeans working in the shops. She now had to walk for 20 minutes to shop for basics.

When Francesca was diagnosed with cancer, she couldn't admit this to her children, but she was partly relieved. The world was changing too much.

ERIC: In the last dialogue Mark, we made the case that angry-nomics is generated every time that the global economy has a major crash. This is a macro story that relates to what we have called *public anger*. Macro crashes release public anger. Macro crashes that are patched up, as was done after the 2008 financial crisis, may suppress that anger, but unless the sources of legitimate public anger are addressed, there is a risk that the system destabilizes and is hijacked by tribalism, which is what we see at the moment.

So now let's turn to *private* anger and angrynomics. Earlier we made a distinction between private and public anger. Private anger tells us about internal stresses that individuals face. Anger in our private lives is indicative of the fact that we are struggling – we seek counseling and help. We are encour-aged to calm down and to address the anger's root causes. In the public sphere moral outrage is something we will defend – it's something we are almost proud of. Public anger seeks a solution to a public wrong. The object of private anger – our family, friends, work colleagues – is rarely the root cause. Private anger seems to be the end of a continuum that starts with stress. In this dialogue we should try to get a sense of what is causing elevated levels of stress, and how this links to the economic causes that are contributing to angrynomics as a personal lived experience.

One idea, which I borrow from psychology and find useful is the notion of *cognitive effort*. Unlike the textbook idea of rational economic agents calculating the best thing to do in every circumstance, real humans struggle the more they have to think, particularly if it is not engaging and creatively rewarding. That is one reason we acquire habits. We get used to the environment we are operating in, and through famili-arity we can achieve a lot without even thinking. This is true at all levels of our daily lives. We put things in places in our houses, so we know how to find them. We learn to drive, so it becomes second nature. We get used to our working environment. We study and train so we have skills that we can often utilize without great effort. Most of what we are doing, most of the time is habitual, learned, behaviour.

Now, the cornerstone of behaviour that is conditioned in this way is the assumption that our environment is not changing. If the world around us changes, our habitual behaviour can misfire, and our skills and background knowledge become redundant. Why do we get stressed when things are not where we think we put them? When we can't visit our local bank, but have to explain everything to someone on a helpline? Why do we resent it when our employer decides to change the layout of our office, or to retrain us?

We do not like changes in our environment. Or rather, change requires cognitive effort, and cognitive effort can be very stressful. Even when it comes to thinking itself, once we have settled on an agreed framework of beliefs – religious, political, scientific, or empirical – we can find it stressful to have that framework challenged or undermined by facts, events, or intellectual challenges, which is part of the reason why social media is so powerful, often unpleasantly aggressive, and self-segregation is so common.

There can be little doubt that the impact of these stressors varies depending on one's age. Babies and young children, encountering the world for the first time, learn and adapt quickly. Give them a phone and they experiment – including by smashing it. The older we are the more vested in learnt practice we become. The elderly often respond to change in our settled environments differently to the young.

In this dialogue I want us to focus on the micro-level

economic and political changes and challenges that have increased the uncertainty in our daily lives. Many of these changes may have aggregate benefits – once we are used to them, they may transform our lives – but constant uncertainty and transitional change can be a significant cause of private stress. In short, I want us to discuss how economic and political changes, driven in part by technology and demography, generate the micro-side of angrynomics.

MARK: I think there are essentially three major causes behind our anxiety and stress: things going wrong in our lives – small things like cars breaking down through to big things like illness and job-loss; not knowing what's happening in our lives, especially uncertainty about the future; and unexpected changes in our environment. Obviously these three factors are all related. Rapid change in our environment creates increased uncertainty and potentially increases the outcomes that may hurt us, in addition to the increased cognitive effort we may need to make as a result.

To help us understand this "micro-side" to angrynomics, I want to first discuss what we mean when we talk about "risk" and "uncertainty" and then look at the economic forces that have contributed to the rapid changes in our environment and increased uncertainty in our lives, some of which may surprise people.

Economists have hijacked the terms "risk" and "uncertainty" by deciding that risk is measurable – you can put a number, a probability, on it – and claiming that uncertainty, which is unknowable, is therefore not worth talking about. This may make economic modeling possible but doing so is quite contrary to what we normally mean by "risk", which is the risk of something going wrong. And when and how the important things go wrong in our lives is often totally unknowable. Bereavement, illness and accidents are among the most stressful events in all our lives and we rarely have any ability to predict when they may strike. They are deeply uncertain, rather than probabilistic.

Take a healthcare example. A cholesterol score of X, in a patient of age Y with weight T, translates into an N percentage chance of a heart attack. If N is high enough, she will be put on statins. Medical practitioners often present this as a measurable probability. But the reality is that there are so many co-founding factors – for example, how much we sleep, drink, our income bracket – to make this a deeply problematic way of thinking.

We like calculations and percentages because they give us the feeling of being in control – we are pricing the probability of an outcome and acting accordingly. But what we are fundamentally uncertain about is whether or not this woman on statins will live to a ripe old age, despite cholesterol, or whether she will be killed driving to work next week by a drunk driver. As Keynes famously quipped about such possibilities, "about these matters there is no scientific basis on which to form any calculable probability whatever. We simply do not know." And that bugs the hell out of us.

A world of measurable probabilities implies a world of free choice. It's a comforting vision. But outside of casinos it's hard to see where such rules apply to the world that we actually inhabit. Most of the choices we make – to buy a house or to rent, to go to one college or course of study over another, what skills to invest in – are not really calculations. We do it because we are born into one family rather than another. We do it for reasons of accident and taste. There is neither a set of prior occurrences we can draw upon to infer probabilities of success or failure, nor is there a stable generator of outcomes producing that world that we can observe and sample.

Skills are another example. Today in the United States, many upper-middle-class families are making their children learn Chinese while also sending them to computer coding camps, which given the way the world is going today seems reasonable. But we also have a strong hunch that many of the jobs that exist today, rightly or wrongly, such as computer coder, are among those most likely to be automated by artificial intelligence. Similarly, the "learn Chinese" option seems to be based upon a notion that by the time these kids grow up China will be running the world economy. But it is equally likely – that is, we have no way of probabilistically estimating that outcome versus any other – that China economically blows up and ends any such possibility. Many parents are then making 15-year bets on their children's futures – and making their summers much less fun – when they have no way of estimating the odds that make them do so.

The generic problem we all face is that major things can go wrong in our lives over which we have very little control. These are usually things that worry us and cause us stress. We hate such uncertainty and try to minimize it. The insurance industry is based upon such minimization – insuring our dependents against our loss of life, protecting us against illness, natural disasters, theft and damage to our property.

Savings perform a similar function. Money is a hedge against possible future states of the world. More broadly, Bar mitzvahs, first communions, marriage ceremonies, the Black–Scholes options pricing formula, and tribal identity all perform the same function: the reduction of uncertainty in our world so that events do not surprise us. Seen in this way, what we discussed in the previous dialogue was not just an economic story. It is just as much a macro-level story about the institutions we build to reduce uncertainty, and how, when such institutions fail, the level of uncertainty we experience rockets, which turns our, if you will, "home-economics" into another source of angrynomics.

ERIC: So, let's complement the macro focus of the third dialogue by dropping down to the micro to examine the more constant, micro-level drivers of uncertainty and insecurity that also generate, not just anger, but the preconditions that give rise to it. While many culprits can be identified, from the growth of the "gig economy" to the increasingly precarious nature of work, four factors in particular seem especially relevant to angrynomics.

The first is the massive changes in the past 30 years which have occurred in product markets, or the different sectors of our economy, including consumer retail, technology, financial services and manufacturing. More intense competition caused by deregulation and rapid technological change translates into more stressful working environments. If businesses are constantly changing or under competitive threat, work is insecure and skills can quickly be made redundant. The Capitalism v.2.0 norm of predictable or stable career paths no longer holds.

The second is the stressor to come – the much-heralded fourth industrial revolution where, according to some reports, up to 60 per cent of all jobs will become automated, and work as we know it will disappear. In the past, technological innovation was framed with optimism for huge improvements in standards of living, today the prevalent narrative seems one of fear and dystopia.

The third micro-stressor is the fact that the populations of developed countries are getting older, which has both short- and long-term consequences for how economies function and how the old stress out the young. The final one – real or imagined – is immigration, a topic which has certainly been used by the media and parts of the political class to fuel tribal anger across much of the developed world. Beyond cynical electoral tactics and scare-mongering to create fictious enemies, it's worth trying to further understand why this has become such an issue and why now.

While all of these micro-level stressors are important, they may not be important for the reasons we commonly think, but collectively they generate a level of near permanent uncertainty that serves as a generator of angrynomics in our daily lives, alongside the anger we have analyzed in the public sphere.

MARK: Let's start with the first one: competition and change in product markets. This is something you've raised with me in many conversations, and which is under-appreciated. The idea that capital faces increased threats and new forms of inse-curity, which are transmitted into pressures in our working lives.

ERIC: Yes, we don't generally think of changes in product markets as a cause of insecurity in our lives, but I think the greatly increased competitive pressures facing the corpo-rate sector have amplified the already strong effects of labour market deregulation and de-unionization that you talked about earlier. As a key cause of increasing private stress, this is under-appreciated. We are all aware of increased job insecu-rity since the 1970s brought about by labour market reforms, particularly in Anglo-Saxon economies. But firms themselves have also experienced accelerating competition, which has done something similar to the corporate sector. Capital as well as labour has become more insecure in important respects.

A great deal of focus has been placed on the emergence of four major tech monopolies in the 2000s – Amazon, Apple, Google and Facebook. But these businesses account for relatively trivial shares of the aggregate employment, and one – Amazon – has done far greater damage to the value of other businesses, largely to the consumer's benefit. There is considerable evidence, particularly with the stability of global inflation, that product market competition in the aggregate has intensified over the past 30 years. This is partly due to policies of deregulation, privatization, and the advent of technology that broke natural monopolies.

The result is that firms in the aggregate are much more likely to be price-takers rather than price-setters, that is, they receive the price that the market gives. Telecommunications is a case in point. A mobile phone provider today takes prices as set by supply and demand. It is not that different to a grain farmer who goes to the market and sells at the market price. If costs go up, it hits profits. Individual firms can't raise prices without customers going to another provider. In contrast, in the 1970s, a national monopolist like British Telecom or AT&T would raise prices when their costs went up, because there was little or no competition.

As we mentioned in the previous dialogue technological and regulatory changes were the micro-side of dismantling the wage-price spiral that crashed Capitalism v.2.0. You can see this very clearly in the effects of price competition across firms, for example, when you analyze the effects of oil price increases on the economy. The correlation between oil prices and inflation was very strong in the 1970s and 1980s. By the mid-1990s it completely breaks down. Today, when the oil price goes up wages and prices often don't move, and even go down. That tells us that product markets are much more competitive than they were in the 1970s, which in turn suggests that there is more going on than the capital versus labour/low wages stressor we discussed in the previous dialogue. There is a capital versus capital dimension, which amplifies this insecurity.

Furthermore, if we are going to identify inequality as one of the bugs that crashed v.3.0, and which still hasn't been adequately dealt with, then we need to accept that there has also been a big increase in inequality – what economists call *dispersion* – within capital itself. And technology is a very important part of this. A lot of the pricing power capital had was because the prevailing technology and the rules of the game in v.2.0 allowed it to play monopoly, which gave those firms steady prices and predictable profits. The policy changes and technology introduced into v.3.0 significantly increased competition, created a wide dispersion of returns between the winners and losers among owners of capital.

Think again about telecoms. As a result of these technological and regulatory changes we all get cheaper telephone calls and digital phones that are powerful computers. When we were children, long-distance calls to relatives or friends were rare, special and brief events. Now we can Skype for free. But whenever we transition from one technological order to another there is an increase in the dispersion of returns, who gets what and how much of it, the creation of new winners and losers, which affects capital as well as workers.

If you were a fixed line operator in the 1990s who had invested in copper wire infrastructure, the value of that capital was destroyed by the shift to mobile technology. Technology has been a huge facilitator of competition and disruption in lots of industries, not just in telecoms, but increasingly in retail and other sectors. So, the inequality we see in income and wealth has a mirror in the returns to capital itself.

This is relevant to private anger because in highly flexible labour markets, firms with razor-thin margins who are extremely price sensitive will have strong incentives not to raise wages, and their survival will require a strong propensity to hire and fire. That goes someway to explaining low wage growth. As more and more sectors are affected by these forces, many of those stresses will be passed on to workers. We see this in the rise of zero-hours contracts in the UK, the rise in minimum-wage jobs, and the growth of platform driven employment such as Task Rabbit and Amazon Mechanical Turk – the so-called "gig economy".

MARK: The particular form technological innovation has taken has also created aggressive price competition. Today's "monopolists" – such as Facebook and Google – provide their products (social media and online search) for *free*, while introducing intense competition in the market for advertising. In the same way that Amazon, through scale economies, has destroyed much of the capital value of traditional retailers. Likewise, social media companies and the internet have substantially damaged the capital value of traditional media industries. The inequality evident in the distribution of the ownership of private wealth has been mirrored in the dispersion between winners and losers within capital.

Recognizing these factors alters our usual interpretation of what's happened in the labour market and gives us an insight into what has been generating insecurity even before the latest crash. While v.3.0 established the trend of income going to capital rather than to labour, and the associated rise in financial leverage compounded this, there was also a huge dispersion of income occurring within capital as a whole that had strong second-order effects on labour. Rapid innovation, scale economies, and competitive markets push down one end of the distribution to be sure, but they also generate big winners at the other end.

What is true for capital has been true for labour. These dynamics are very clear in the sports industry, with the top clubs and stars taking the majority of the spoils. Take English football, which is today globally consumed. The number of Manchester United fans today lies in the millions and they can all pay to watch their team play (or steal the game via streaming – more tech disruption), whereas in the 1940s and 1950s, only 70,000 fans – the capacity at Old Trafford – were able to see their team play. Today, there is no such constraint. Given this, Manchester United is now fantastically profitable, despite its results. But only a few clubs can do this. There are 92 clubs in English football's top four leagues, but there is only room for a handful of Manchester United-type teams. The result is a handful of really big winners with quasi-monopoly status at the top, and a very long tail with everyone else earning a fraction of their returns. If you take this as a model of what is happening in sectors everywhere, you can see that most people are going to be in that long tail with the low returns.

ERIC: So, it is very clear that uncertainty and insecurity in our working lives have increased in ways that are disconcerting and stressful. The root causes in de-unionization and labour market deregulation have been reinforced by competitive pressures and technological change in product markets. What about the much publicized "gig economy" – is this relevant?

MARK: Yes it is, but a look at the data complicates this argument in an interesting way. US labour market data reveal that the much commented upon "Uberization" of the low end of the labour market hasn't actually happened, at least not in the way and to the extent that we expect. There were actually less people employed in so-called "contingent" work arrangements in 2017 than in 1995. Indeed, going by the standard definition of employment, fully 96 per cent of the market is not Uberized. Moreover, if you are in that four per cent, you are likely to be better paid than those in comparable jobs in the 96 per cent. But part of the problem here is definitional. The US Bureau of Labor Statistics (BLS) only counts a worker as "contingently" employed if their primary income comes from contingent work. But there are many more workers who supplement their stagnant wages in other sectors by joining in the gig economy. So the figure is recomputed to around 10 per cent and may be higher. But the fact remains that most workers are not in contingent employment. So how then do we understand the self-reported data on how workers feel about their employment being insecure?

A moment from the UK Brexit campaign may help us understand how the deeper forces of insecurity we have identified matters more than the gig economy. During the Brexit campaign, "Remain" campaigners visited Newcastle in the north-east of England to debate the impact of Britain leaving the EU. During the visit one of the Remain spokesmen opined to his audience that if the Leave campaign won, GDP would fall. From the back of the hall came the reply, "your GDP, not ours!", which was met with bemused looks from the podium. After all, GDP applies to the economy as a whole, it's not divisible.

But what that worker was getting at was the essence of

what we have been getting at in this dialogue. Nissan's profits and sales are up, but that worker's wages are not rising. Every successive contract signed cuts worker benefits, regulates bathroom breaks, stretches shifts. Management repeatedly tell their workers that unless targets are met the plant will have to close and production will shift to France. They then tell the workers in the French plant the same thing, but that their jobs will go to Romania. Given this, GDP may be increasing, but only a fraction of it is coming back to the workers generating it, the majority is going to stockholders, who don't live in Sunderland and who don't work for Nissan. So why not vote against the system that makes this possible?

Globalization, technological change, margin suppression, the reclassification of employees as contractors as firms face stiffer competition, and the intensification of competition all increase the uncertainty felt by workers, even in supposedly well-paid and secure employment. One does not have to be a member of the precariat to feel precarious. And feeling precarious as a permanent state is a giant insecurity generator.

ERIC: Technology plus deregulation is then a stressor on all of us. Heightened competition, more "flexible" contracts, repeated pressure on wages is a constant rather than a variable for many people. But technology has also become a serious stressor over recent years in a much more unusual way. That is, stories about what technology will do to us in the future turn out to affect us now in the present. Here's what I mean.

Remember what we said about risk and uncertainty? Ideas about likely future states of the world that become dominant are causally important in bringing that future about. Think about Bitcoin for a moment. It is neither a store of value nor a unit of exchange, nor a unit of account, so it's not money. But because people think that it will be the money *of the future*, fortunes are won and lost trading it. I want to suggest that how we think about emerging technologies has that character and that doing so has, over the past decade, added a whole layer of uncertainty to our lives.

Concerns over technology replacing jobs are as old as capitalism itself. And yet, despite all those concerns, from the followers of Ned Ludd (the original "Luddite") in the early nineteenth century who broke weaving machines to save hand-weavers' jobs, to the "Race Against the Machine" crowd at MIT today, the fact remains that every time there has been a major technological shift the demand for labour has increased, not decreased. And while the neo-Luddites who focus on the future effects of artificial intelligence (AI) and machine learning (ML) maintain that "this time it's different", there is actually remarkably little evidence that this is the case. Indeed, what actual evidence we have so far suggests that not only will automation increase employment, but that we absolutely need the productivity gains digital automation will bring over the next 20–30 years as societies age or we will become much poorer and angrier than we are now.

MARK: Here's something that perhaps illustrates this tension for people who lived through the 2010s. Just as the global financial crisis really began to bite in Europe in 2010, the press everywhere suddenly became replete with stories about how pretty much all workers were shortly to be replaced by robots. Whether in the form of self-driving cars and trucks, drone delivery of goods, computer analysis of financial and legal data, blockchain and bitcoin, we were told over and over that no one was immune. Why? Because this time it was different – different in that AI and ML would combine to do things better

102

than humans can do, and that such machines would get better at doing whatever they do better faster than we can catch up, hence the "race against the machine" and we were all going to lose.

So where were we in the race? We needed numbers, and they were duly supplied. An early study from Oxford University estimated that almost half of all US jobs could be automated within ten years. The Bank of England later reduced that number to a third. The OECD then took it down to 9 per cent, as reality took hold.[24] That is, once the hysteria died down, certain things started to become apparent.

The first was that almost none of these technologies either exist or are deployable at scale. Self-driving cars and trucks are probably the most developed of these technologies, but they only exist in pilot schemes and are subject to innumerable legal and practical obstacles. Think about the following problem. How do you write a computer command in advance to tell the self-driving car to "always hit the car with fewer people in it" in order to minimize losses, and not get sued by the family of the fewer people in the car? Nonetheless, the constant drumbeat that, for example, in a decade "all truck-driving jobs will go the way of the gas-lighter" may be, in part, responsible for the fact that the US trucking industry was by around 2017 short of 100,000 drivers and the fleet was operating at 100 per cent capacity. After all, if the job will disappear tomorrow, why invest in getting a licence today? As Keynes said, depress expectations today, get less investment tomorrow.

Second, while some aspects of almost all jobs can be automated, even ours, not every part of a job can be decomposed. Consider that the fastest growing category of job by volume of jobs produced in the US today is elder care nurse/home help/

nursing assistant. Despite the efforts of many Japanese firms, there is no robot for taking care of Grandma – nor do most people want one. As we've discussed, the mere existence of a technology does not make it a success. Demand drives supply. Tech boosters and neo-Luddites assume the opposite.

Third, while AI and ML are real and are different, as seen in the success of products such as Amazon's Alexa and Google's AlphaGo engine, it's not clear that their deployment at scale, which is still a long way off, is zero-sum against either workers or wages. Take AI and power grid optimization. An intelligent programme monitoring and optimizing flow across a carbon-smart grid could save huge amounts of energy, reduce costs for all firms and households, and help with climate change. At least some of those savings would show up in cheaper products and demand for new goods and services, not all of which can be done by robots.

What we should really care about then are the returns to robot-makers. That is, we don't want a situation where ownership of critical technologies creates a tiny class of trillionaire investors who earn monopoly profits while the rest of us eat gruel. While such an outcome is a possibility, the mere existence of states, elections and democracy act as limits to such accumulation. But even here, what evidence we do have is that robots increase productivity, which in turn increases employment. Let me give you an example I know personally.

There is a prosciutto firm in Rhode Island called Daniele Inc., that a decade ago employed around 200 people. When the sons took over from the father, they looked at the process of making prosciutto and decided to make it more efficient. They decided to build a big new factory and to bring in as many robots as possible. Doing so caused a 20 per cent cut in their workforce as many of the workers who moved the hams around were made redundant. Ten years later the firm employs over 800 people and is poised to open a new factory.

The robots replaced the type of labour that causes chronic back injury and disability. The company's profit margins rose as their costs fell and they were able to increase production, selling into more markets, making different products. The robots may have cost 40 people their jobs, but they made possible 600 new ones. Meanwhile, more people than ever eat prosciutto. Unless you're a pig, it's not clear how the robots are the bad guys here. Indeed, that level of productivity enhancement is exactly what we need to stay wealthy amidst demographic change.

Given all this, while technology may be a micro-stressor insofar as it heightens competition, it's far from clear that these emerging technologies will ever do many of the bad things already priced in as happening to us. Robots and associated technologies may put further downward pressure on wages in the future, but we should not blame something that doesn't exist today for already having effects. But in a weird way we have done just that.

Right in the midst of a giant banking-induced implosion and consequent recession, several *years* of news items across the world told labour, especially semi-skilled labour, that its days were numbered.[25] At a time where inequality and unfairness and the cry that "the system is rigged" had become hot-button political issues, it also seemed that the very people who got bailed out were about to make the biggest killing of all by permanently depriving the folks who didn't get rescued of their livelihoods by replacing them all with robots.

The tragedy of this coincidence is not just how it increases the uncertainty and anger of individuals, but how it links into the other stressors we want to talk about, which are aging and immigration. With the whole world getting older and with immigration being increasingly contested, unless you are able to embrace technological change and augment productivity, you are definitely about to get a lot more stressed out.

ERIC: Here's how angrynomics, technology and aging all come together in a particular generational politics. In late 2016 the US Congress passed a law at the behest of Joe Biden, the then outgoing vice president, who lost his son to brain cancer, to do a "Cancer Moonshot". Congress found $6.2 billion to fund advanced research to get drugs to market more quickly. Now that's great, except that Congress also has a law that says if you want to spend new money, and you don't raise taxes for it, then it must be appropriated from an existing part of the budget. Where did they take it from? Mainly from preventative care programmes. Now ask yourself the following question: who gets cancer? It's typically not healthy 35 or 45-year-olds like Biden's son – it's old people. And who benefits from preventative care? It's basically the young. This is an inter-generational transfer. We just don't see this for what it is.

MARK: We saw something analogous in Greece. Around the same time as Biden's moonshot was being put together the left-wing Greek government was embroiled with its creditors about a "13th month" payment to pensioners. Given that Greece had been battered with mindless austerity programmes, GDP had shrunk by a quarter, and pensions in some cases had fallen by up to 30 per cent, you can understand why they might want to resist these cuts. But do factor this in too, which is as true in Greece as it is everywhere else: pensioners are twice as likely to vote as the young and so politicians pay disproportionate attention to them. Also remember that in 1950, 12.5 per cent of the population of Europe were of pension age. Today its

25 per cent. So, these days potentially half the voting public are pensioners. Now, guess which group within Greek society has the lowest rate of poverty? Pensioners. Indeed, poverty among the young unemployed is four to five times the rate among pensioners in Greece, despite the cuts. Greece could have distributed to the young, but they chose to protect the old. This is, once again, an inter-generational transfer.

ERIC: I will give you another one. The British National Health Service is a national treasure that costs a fortune. As British society gets older, it will cost more and more. Now, in a seemingly different area entirely, the British government quietly privatized the UK's higher education system after the financial crisis, introducing tuition fees of approximately £9,000 a year. But if the state is no longer subsidizing higher education, where did all those savings go? They went to the NHS. Now, who consumes healthcare resources? Is it the young, or the old?

MARK: In all of these cases we are seeing a very quiet, but hugely significant, series of inter-generational transfers, which matter not just because across rich countries the old dominate politics. Perhaps more importantly, it is the old that have most of the assets. The US data tell an interesting story here. Eighty per cent of all financial assets are owned by "Baby Boomers" (those born between 1945 and 1964). But it's also true that half of all boomers have no retirement assets, and that only 22 per cent of private retirement accounts in the US have any cash or cash-earning assets such as stocks and shares in them, all of which tells us that there is incredible inequality among boomers as a group. This inequality shows up in the fact that of those 80 per cent of financial assets, 80 per cent (64 per cent of the total) are owned by the top 20 per cent of boomers.[26] How did they get so rich?

The US Federal Reserve has some research that explains why some boomers ended up making off with almost all the cash. Firstly, they received a massive capital endowment legacy from the people who came before them. The parents of the boomers – the so-called "Greatest Generation" – paid very high taxes and invested massively in infrastructure and education in the immediate aftermath of the Second World War, which their kids, the boomers, got for free. Then the boomers themselves had fewer kids.

Now if economic growth is determined primarily by technology and demography – the number of workers times the number of hours worked plus the amount of capital with which they work – the boomers arrived in a sweet spot where it was hard not to grow really fast. But because the boomers had fewer kids, the demographic component of growth fell at the same time as they accumulated more and more assets. As such, the rate of capital formation, a core determinant of investment, is slowing as the dependency ratio – the ratio of workers to retirees – is shifting over time, which in turn slows future growth, while still compounding the massive amount of assets that those "top twenty" boomers have accumulated already.

ERIC: This is why, at least in part, the economist Thomas Piketty thinks that intergenerational inequality is a necessary part of our future, unless we choose to do something about it. Piketty's book, *Capital in the Twenty-First Century*, is famous for putting inequality back on the political agenda in a serious way. But his book is as much about economic growth as it is inequality. Piketty's framework for thinking about economic growth allows us to see the long-run consequences of these observations about aging.

Pretty much all economics that seeks to explain growth begins with what's called the Solow growth model, which says that output is a function of the number of workers, multiplied by the amount of capital, plus available technology. Because of capital depreciation (stuff wears out and needs to be replaced) and population growth being constant in the short run, technological change is the key thing that moves us from one state to another – and that "movement" is growth. However, technology is "exogenous" – it is outside the model.

Piketty revises that model in a way that makes a lot of sense for where we are today. Rather than making technology exogenous, he takes it as fixed in the short run – another app on your smartphone is not a serious technological shift. What he makes variable instead is population. Specifically, demography and aging. When you do this, you are effectively asking the following question: how does an economy of old people, who will work less and less over time, but who hold most of the investible assets behave?

The standard model of consumption through the human life cycle assumes that you are asset poor when you're young, so you borrow. Then in your mid-life, you have a combination of both assets you are accumulating and debts you are reducing. Then in the latter part of the cycle you have few or no debts, more assets, and you run down those assets as consumption in your retirement. But this is a very partial description of reality. There are unexpected and pernicious side-effects.

Firstly, as the Fed research points out, an economy of old people will grow more slowly. The US population is still comparatively young, but your average Italian and Japanese is 47 years old. It is wholly implausible that an elderly population will have a high rate of consumption *growth*. And without that you cannot expect these economies to grow much at all.

Second, if the assets owned by that generation are highly concentrated, then what Piketty calls a new "patrimonial capitalism" arises that compounds the problem. If the top 20 per cent of boomers owns a huge chunk of everything, they can spend as much as they want in retirement, end-of-life care, and still pass on huge endowments to their children, which is unmeritocratic and keeps inequality structurally high. In short, aging itself becomes a regenerator of inequality across the generations at the same time as slowing growth overall.

MARK: Given all that, now think again about those transfers in the US, Greece, and the UK across generations due to policy, and you end up with a world where liabilities are distributed towards young people while the assets are distributed disproportionately towards the old, and unless they are rich enough to leave them to their own children, the life cycle model, and intergenerational asset formation, totally breaks down. And since politicians respond primarily to money and the votes of the over 55s, you know that this trend will continue.

This then is our third stressor, after inequality in returns and technological disruption – what aging does to capitalist economies. An economy where the young have all the liabilities and a fraction of the old have all the assets is a deeply stressful one. Unless you are lucky by birth, your ability to form assets over the life cycle is seriously impaired while your taxes will be used to pay for the old who weren't in the top 20 per cent of the income distribution. We see this already in a myriad of ways. In the US, boomers went to college basically for free, whereas millennials in the US have $1.7 trillion in student loans. The Trump tax cuts handed out, guess what, $1.5 trillion dollars to, primarily the rich, the vast majority of whom are old.

If you are young and are paying back student loans you are not saving for a mortgage, which is why millennials are postponing buying a house and other major purchases. Given stagnant wages, high debts, increased competition, and a future where they are constantly told they will be replaced by technology, add in the unwillingness of boomer-age politicians to do much about climate change and is it any wonder that young people are especially disaffected from traditional political parties and institutions? The old do not stress the young deliberately. And 80 per cent of US boomers may be as poor as many millennials. But structurally, aging, plus low growth, plus low wages, plus debt, leads to a stressful place. One that cries out for a target, and increasingly that target seems to be immigration. So, let's talk about that.

ERIC: We have seen in our discussion of tribal rage just how easy it is to trigger the human instinct to latch on to fictious "identities" in order to form groups or tribes, and how easily this instinct can turn into rage and then violence. My strong belief is that immigration is primarily an issue that the media and political class have hijacked to suit their interests. Tell me why I should think otherwise?

MARK: I want to draw upon two examples – how immigration played into the Brexit vote and the German reaction to Syrian refugees – to shed light on this question. I then want to make a claim – that how immigration is subjectively experienced varies across the income distribution – and then tie those observations together to suggest that immigration is both the political lightening rod for the tribal version of angrynomics while being a legitimate concern that needs to be addressed if we want the world to be less angry.

For me the refrain that "the Brexit referendum was not about economics" is based on the fact that there was no obvious one-to-one correlation between the level of income of a given constituency and the desire to vote leave. This much is true. But it is also partial. Voting leave correlated with lower skill levels, which are a proxy for income, as well as hourly earnings, population density (cities are richer than towns and villages) and competition from imports, and a host of other economic negatives.

What a deeper analysis of Brexit revealed was that the real action was in the rate of change in a variable rather than in its absolute values. What Brexit voting showed us was that while it was true that the absolute level of income did not matter, what did matter was how income had shifted over time. If an area saw a relative downward shift in income or house prices over a sustained period of time, and at the same time it experienced a rise in the number of migrants, then that area, especially if it was rural, was likely to vote to leave.[27]

Economics and immigration were then inseparable. If you think your environment is slowly getting worse over time, while immigrants are coming in, it's almost inevitable that this correlation – house prices down, foreigners up – will be turned into a causal statement that "I am getting worse off relatively because 'they' are coming in". And the more of an identifiable group "they" are, the easier it is to do this and capitalize upon it if you are a populist politician.

Moreover, it is uncomfortable for people like us who support immigration to recognize it is a real stressor *in its own right* and not just as a tribal reaction and a political tactic. And that's because one's lived experience of immigration, therefore one's fear of it, varies across the income distribution.

For example, we sit squarely in the top five per cent of the income distribution. And for us, immigration is a wonderful thing. The immigrants that we meet are likely to be just like us. They may have an advanced degree, or work for a company, just like us. Their kids will go to the same school as ours. Nothing this immigrant family consumes detracts from our consumption. They contribute to the economy as we do. Lower income, less educated and less cosmopolitan immigrants live nowhere near me, they cannot afford to, and I can consume the services and goods that they produce as I please.

Now consider someone at the bottom of the income distribution, someone in the bottom ten per cent, in Germany to be specific. That person is likely to reside in public housing. For the past two decades they have been told how their condition is their fault. How we all need to spend less on welfare. How there is no money for them, for their tribe.

And then there is a humanitarian crisis in Syria and the leadership in your country says "we can do this", and decides to take in a million or more people who the media repeatedly tell you are quite different from you and your tribe. You then discover that money is plentiful, but that it's definitely not available for your tribe – it's for "them" – or at least that's what you hear in the media each day. Scarce public housing is to be directed towards this new group. Job training, language training, new schools and teachers, it's all possible, but it's not for you or your tribe.

For people like us in the top five per cent this is a non-event and so I don't suffer the costs of this humanitarianism. I am not competing for public housing, or training, nor am I in a low-income job that can easily be done by someone else. But for those in the bottom ten per cent, whose claims to goods are delegitimated further, they see immigration as a threat.

This is pretty much what happened in Germany when, in 2015, Chancellor Merkel faced with a humanitarian crisis developing on Germany's borders said "Wir schaffen das" – basically "we can (and should) do this". The electoral result of doing so, a year and a bit later, was the worst showing at the polls in decades for Merkel's party and the rise of an explicitly anti-immigration party called the Alternative für Deutschland, the AfD.

Angrynomics is fully apparent when one looks at the vote for the AfD. Germany is a country rich in resources, and is well-governed in the main, so if anyone could take in a million refugees it would be them. They also had the sense to allot refugees to areas that had the capacity to support them, primarily in the south and south-west – the richest parts of the country.

But that is not where the AfD found their voice. That was in the poorest part of the country – in the north-east, in the former East Germany – where there were almost no migrants. Indeed, the number one predictor of voting AfD was the same as we saw in the Brexit referendum. If you have been in relative decline for a long time, as East Germany and parts of rural England have been, you were primed for an anti-immigrant response. Indeed, if you lived in an area in the former East where there were virtually no immigrants, and you were old, then your vote for the AfD was pretty much guaranteed. You can then have a reaction against immigrants even in areas where there are none, because what is being priced-in is the media-infected politically turbocharged narrative that this is going to cost me what little I have.

In communities such as these, immigration is seen as a stressor that pushes against those already most affected by technological change, competition, stagnant wages, and the downsides of aging with no assets. Indeed, researchers who have studied immigration for a long time have known forever that immigration has long been unpopular with the majority of the citizens of western nations.[28] Pro-immigration forces, tended to be wealthier and bore no downside costs from being pro-immigrant. Ignoring the asymmetric benefit and costs of migraton makes for an easier politics. It's easier to chastise the poor for their racism than to do anything about their poverty. But if we do want to do something about angrynomics, we need to take this stressor seriously too.

ERIC: I think you point to very real beliefs that people hold, which one needs to take account of, even if there are strong arguments to the contrary. But I think we need to think harder about why now, and why this subject, has become so contested. If I think how it has been raised in the British political context, I think there is deep hypocrisy, cynicism and a decidedly pernicious undercurrent that is being manipulated for political advantage, to disguise a very real unwillingness to tackle regional economic development, low incomes and public service provision.

There is a lot of serious empirical research into the economic effects of immigration. The main bone of contention is whether immigration has adversely affected wages at the lower end of the spectrum. The data is inconclusive. I suspect the story varies with circumstance. It seems obvious, for example, that agricultural labourers from eastern Europe working on the farms in the East of England have depressed the wages of those already working on the farms. But the reality is far more complex. The revival of agriculture due to the arrival of cheap labour has actually supported regional economic growth and coincided with steep *declines* in the unemployment rate. It's also what is keeping those small rural towns in business.

There are scenarios where immigration ends up regenerating, creating new jobs, and as a result, creating higher wages. There are parts of northern England where this looks like an accurate description of reality, and yet towns, such as Boston in rural Lincolnshire, voted overwhelmingly to leave the EU. The share of those voting leave among pensioners and social welfare recipients in these localities was also higher than the average across all leave voters. This is inconsistent with an argument based on economic interest. From a policy perspective, if we want to address low wages or inequality, we would focus on taxation, provision of public services and macro-policies to ensure tight labour markets. I am not at all convinced that immigration is behind either low wages or inequality.

I'd rather put it this way. The political identities fostered by Capitalism v.2.0 (left versus right) and v.3.0 (liberal cosmopolitanism) were historical oddities. Version 2.0's identities lost their relevance with the shift from v.2.0 to v.3.0 and the end of the Cold War. The essentially content-free liberal cosmopolitanism that took its place in v.3.0 was sustainable only until the system that supported it crashed. At that moment, nationalism, based upon the exploitation of increased uncertainty by elites and the media, driven by tribalism, and catalysed and amplified by political opportunists, fills the void. The combined stressors of the crash, competition, technological change (real and imagined) and the downsides of aging are given voice in that moment, and in one form, that voice turns against immigrants.

MARK: Let's bring all this together. There are two faces of public anger. The first is a tribal energy, a motivating and potentially violent strain of our instinct to form groups that is associated with our fears, threats, and a worldview which is decidedly zero-sum. The tribal anger we are witnessing today predates the most recent global economic traumas, although they have accelerated its force.

We have also emphasized a second, totally different side to anger, anger as an expression of a legitimate voice, which has genuine grievances and has not been listened to. We have identified a series of fundamental economic triggers, devastating cyclical mismanagement of the economy, especially in Europe, extremes in wealth and income inequality, a neutering of the nation state under globalization, a corrupted financialized elite using crises as an opportunity to bypass democratic process.

An irony is that Capitalism v.3.0 contributed to these pathologies by eroding political identity and in doing so it ultimately revealed its own deep economic flaws. The political classes – bereft of ideas – are now desperately peddling old ideologies and instincts, or pursuing bizarre distractions, like Brexit. We have put all this into the historic context of the last 70 years, using an analogy of capitalist hardware, an ideas-based operating system, and an inevitable bug-inflicted systems failure – the crash revealing which emperors were naked.

Private anger, the subject of this dialogue, is a very different species, but it is the micro-side of the macro version of angrynomics we discussed in Dialogue 3. In contrast to moral outrage in the public sphere, private anger reveals something internal. It is not a reason-based call for legitimate rebalancing. Kicking one's car out of frustration rarely signals a demand for electric motors. The fundamental question is why are we so stressed? Especially, when on the face of it "we have never had it so good". Stress is primarily caused by things going wrong, but also by uncertainty and change. Specifically, technological changes, demographic changes, increased insecurity due to deregulation and liberalization, an absence of voice, and increasing inequality.

Anger, as a theme, unites the public and private, the macro and micro. It helps us make sense of political developments that otherwise appear chaotic and frightening. It also gives us a guide to what to listen to, what to contain, and hopefully what action to take. In the real world of course, these factors are interacting to create what you and I have termed angrynomics. The question now is: what do we do to reduce the anger? Ultimately, we are trying to rewrite the software, so what do we need to do?

ERIC: In previous eras that we've talked about there was always a set of competing policies, ready and waiting. After the failure of v.1.0, in the 1930s and 1940s, there emerged a set of mixed-economy Keynesian ideas ready to be implemented. After the failure of v.2.0 the free-market economists Milton Friedman and Friedrich Hayek provided Thatcher and Reagan with a new software manual. Today, functional finance, a left-wing version of Friedman and Abba Lerner, has been revived as a fringe ideology in the US under the misnomer, modern monetary theory (MMT), but in practice there appears to be no serious ideological parallel in the current era with which to reboot angrynomics.

We believe that we have serious problems, but there is no clear sense of "okay, here are the policies to go for based upon these new ideas", which reinforces the space for regressive tribal politics. The era of anodyne centrism has left us not only bereft of motivating political identities, but also, it seems, bereft of useful new ideas. What ideas there are tend back to the national state, and perhaps there is a reason for that.

Consider that every time the system has a crash and reset, every time something really disrupts the system, the container of hopes becomes the nation state, for good or ill. When we sat together in London in the summer of 2016 we saw Jeremy Corbyn, the leader of the UK's Labour Party, giving a very weak-kneed defence of the EU during the Brexit campaign. The governing Conservatives had dealt themselves a post-Brexit political agenda that was all about taking back control – us against them – the national against the international. The 2019 British elections demonstrated this further, with both the major parties promising renewal centred around national control, although giving it quite different content (Brexit versus state ownership). Trump's economic nationalism is a capitalist variant. Scottish nationalism is a left-wing version. All these perspectives appear at one level as cynical attempts to deflect attention away from a disconcerting, complex and uncertain reality with a simplistic and comforting return to tribal flag-waving. All that is wrong is global, cosmopolitan, or market-driven. If only we could revert back to the local, the national, the knowable – to the "us" of the nation. So, my question is this: can we use the "default setting" of the nation to address the drivers of angrynomics, without succumbing to the darker instincts of nationalism?

MARK: My instincts and my analysis say "yes", and the reason lies in the system failure at the heart of current macroeconomic policy across the world. Quite simply, having handed all the levers of policy to central banks, they now appear to be saying, "we've done all we can, over to you". Now why is there a crisis in the regime of technocrats? Well, firstly, just as they pronounced their greatest achievement, the so-called "Great Moderation", which eliminated the business cycle, the wheels truly fell off the wagon and we had the most severe recession since the Great Depression.

But there also seems to be another problem that has come

to the fore in the last three to four years, which is that interest rates don't seem to work anymore. Increasingly, the central banks are declaring their impotence. Whereas the entire governing ideology had been, "Don't worry, interest rates always work. Inflation is always and everywhere a monetary phenomenon", that now appears to be asymmetric. We may sometimes live in an inflationary world, such as the 1960s and 1970s, where inflation was accommodated with money supply growth, but when we get deflation, like in Japan, or in Europe, where inflation has been below target for a long period of time, the central banks seem ineffective. It appears that the hither-to policy tool of choice – interest rates – may be *hardware-dependent*.

ERIC: Let me clarify that. Think of the crisis Kalecki predicted would happen in v.2.0 – a crisis of inflation. Monetary policy plays a big role in the reset of that system. To kill inflation, the Fed, the Bundesbank, the Bank of England could all jack up interest rates very aggressively and, as long as you had political cover, that would kill inflation. Now the irony is that just as the 1970s stagflation was relatively unique in capitalist history, so were the relatively high real interest rates that prevailed at the end of this era when inflation was crushed.

Given this, we start in the mid-1980s with very high levels of real interest rates, and very low levels of debt, which had been inflated away in the prior decade. From that point onwards, every time there was a cyclical problem there was plenty of room to cut interest rates. Central banks had huge mone-tary power to unleash with lower interest rates, which was their response to every recession in the subsequent 20 years. The result was 20 years of reasonable success. But every time interest rates are cut, we lose the scope to ease further, and the leverage starts to rise. Eventually you get to zero, or even slightly negative, and the game is up.

The 2008 financial crash and the monetary policy response has caused a deep crisis in this policy framework and we've discovered that we hadn't eliminated recessions after all. The tragedy is that we gave over all powers of macro policy-making to central banks to use interest rates to determine everything, and now we're saying, "no, we still have cycles and, oh, the single lever that we built our institutions and intellectual framework (interest rates) around no longer works". We need to get past this framework of governing the economy, and there are good reasons for doing so.

But there is an upside if this is the case. Kalecki's pessimism that it all has to end in an inflationary nightmare of class con-flict doesn't appear to be the inevitable fate it once was. We now have large parts of the developed world where unemployment has reached 40-year lows and there is no inflation. In some parts of the world, such as central and eastern Europe, inflation is also proving to be relatively unaffected by high wage growth.

Something new has happened, which must prompt a fundamental rethink: we have a combination of close to full employment with interest rates so low that without new tools central banks are impotent. If you believe in the importance of preventing recessions, which we do, this has to be addressed. At the same time we have two problems which are crying out for direct, powerful and compelling policy responses: climate change and inequality. The centre of politics cannot hold. It has no ideas on either of these most pressing issues.

We need to address the deep-seated source of legitimate anger, which neoliberal ideology brushed under the carpet and has been brutally revealed in the post-crisis regime. We need to simultaneously unleash the productivity potential of technological change to cope with the challenges of demography and aging, while addressing extreme and corrupting inequality of wealth and income. We also need to revisit the labour market – can we keep the benefits of deregulation, but mitigate or eliminate the stressors?

We agree that the supposed impotence of central banks in a world of low interest rates, is in fact a huge opportunity, both for a more effective monetary policy and for a smart expansion of the state's balance sheet. The unexpected post-crisis success of high employment, no inflation, and negative real interest rates in fact frees government up to make some critical interventions. So, in our next dialogue let's explain how, and propose some concrete radical policies that will work to reduce the anger powering angrynomics. If the modern tribalists are rogue code writers, then we can have a go too.

DIALOGUE 5

Calming the anger: from angrynomics to an economics that works for everyone

"Anger is a valid emotion. It's only bad when it takes control and makes you do things you don't want to do."
ELLEN HOPKINS

The parable of the good father turned populist

We first met John in March 2009. He was working as a waiter in an upmarket restaurant in Naples, Florida. We struck up a conversation. John is Irish-American, originally from Boston, he had recently moved to Florida with his family. His girls had grown up, been through college, and had found jobs. Only his youngest was still living with him and his wife. They had moved to Florida looking forward to a peaceful retirement. The kids could visit in the winter months and escape to the sunshine.

Several months prior, John's youngest daughter was diagnosed with a very rare, but life-threatening, heart condition. Eventually, after many hospital visits, John learnt that there was only one specialist with sufficient expertise and the right technology to help his daughter. The heart surgeon was world-renowned and worked for the Miami Dolphins. John sought, and received, his help. His daughter was operated on and made a swift recovery. She is now a healthy 20-something. But John is saddled with over a million dollars of debt. That's why, approaching his seventies, he is still working.

When we first spoke to John, in 2009, he was angry. All over the news were reports of bonuses being paid to executives at a huge American insurance company called AIG that went bankrupt. John had done most things right in his life. He had played by the rules. He had paid his taxes. He was a good husband and a good father. Right at the end of his working life, all his plans were thrown in the air. He accepted that. His daughter's health came first. That was never in doubt. But these guys had cheated. They had bankrupted their firm, which the government – taxpayers like him – had to bailout, or it would, so we were told, destroy the whole financial system. Usually, this would be called extortion. These guys were lucky to escape jail. But worse, they were due to receive bonuses so extravagant that one year's worth would clear all the debts he had incurred to pay for his daughter's medical bills. John is soft-spoken. He is a mild-mannered man. Not one to lose his temper or start an argument. But something about what he was experiencing made him angry. He felt cheated. He had been lied to. And nothing was being done about it.

╫ ╫ ╫

MARK: In the previous two dialogues we described how the earlier versions of capitalism crashed causing much public anger, and how more micro-level changes also reproduced and amplified that anger at a private level. In this dialogue, let's turn to solutions. The first question to ask when we look at repairing or replacing the software on the reboot of v.3.0 is what do we need? Let's start this discussion by identifying the bits of v.3.0 that despite its failure are worth keeping. And from there we can discuss our new code and explain why it is needed to prevent angrynomics from boiling over into something even more pernicious.

ERIC: For all v.3.0's faults and terminal crash, most folks do not want to start completely from scratch. The costs of doing so are high and attempts to do so tend to end badly. So, what can we keep from the old model and build on? To me, the best model of v.3.0 is probably something close to what the Australians managed to achieve.

The great achievement of v.3.0 was the control of inflation and the apparently successful fix of the virus that Kalecki identified – that sustained full employment would inevitably create a wage-price inflation spiral. Version 3.0 has succeeded in delivering a very prolonged period of near-full employment without inflationary pressures. This may be due to deregulated labour markets, but we have also argued that highly competitive product markets, global competition and technology are important forces. But despite these forces, some economies, such as Australia, have had very decent real wage growth and they have not seen inflation problems for the past 30 years. Unemployment in 2019 had fallen to levels not seen since the 1960s in many parts of the developed world, and the lowest levels in decades in parts of central and eastern Europe. In many of these economies real wage growth is now strong. So much so that Australia no longer looks like an outlier. Relative cyclical stability – what you and I have called *secular stability* – looks obtainable and can produce consistently tight labour markets.

What Australia got right, and Canada too, was to have heavily regulated their banks ahead of the financial crisis. Now this is no panacea, but it's a good place to start. The rest of the world needed to learn this lesson. The policies of the 1980s did succeed in stabilizing inflation. But instability eventually emerged in highly leveraged financial institutions. These financial institutions assumed there would never be another recession and leveraged their balance sheets to maximize profits and fundamentally created the crisis. If things go wrong, leverage kills. And it did – big time.

The lesson the world over is that banks need high capital and liquidity ratios. They need financial buffers to protect themselves against bad loans and attempts by businesses and households to build cash holdings during a panic. As a result of far more aggressive regulation since the crisis, banks are no longer allowed to run with huge balance sheet risk. It should not surprise anyone that inflation has remained dead, but for more than a decade since we required global banks to raise capital and liquidity ratios to high levels, there has been one of the longest uninterrupted phases of growth in the United States, and increasingly, elsewhere.

Full employment and financial stability are significant achievements. Although there is still a lot of hand-wringing about the financial sector in particular, and calls, notably by some around Trump, encouraging him to let the banks loose again, the lesson and practice is pretty clear – low inflation and heavy regulation of banks can deliver very prolonged phases of full employment and secular stability. It is very important to understand these achievements. If sustained, this is a big deal. Particularly if it coincides with very low real interest rates.

The death of inflation has also permitted much more aggressive counter-cyclical demand management, something which many reformers seem oblivious to. It is a profound irony that the policies introduced in the 1980s in response to a perceived failing of Keynesian economics, actually made Keynesian demand management much more possible.

MARK: Explain what you mean, without the jargon, why secular stability is so important and why Keynesian v.2.0 solutions are now more rather than less possible.

ERIC: First, we have the facts. The policies of the 1980s and 1990s, of globalization, deregulation of product and labour markets, destroyed inflation. The reason many economists and politicians heralded "no more boom and bust" was therefore somewhat understandable. The experience of the 1970s taught them that inflation was the main source of recessions. And in many lower-income economies – like Turkey, India, Brazil and South Africa – inflation still is a major problem that critically prevents them from stopping recessions by easing fiscal and monetary policy.

Of course, as is now obvious, although policy-makers were right to herald the control of inflation they forgot about the second source of major instability: the financial sector. Worse still, they ignored the risk that in response to great economic stability due to the control of inflation, the private sector would take on more financial risk, and eventually this would be hugely destabilizing. The severity of the crash was in part a reflection of success.

Having relearnt the lessons of economic history, it is important to take stock. We need to maintain the heavy regulation of banks that has been hard won. But we don't want to re-regulate the rest of the private sector and bring back Kalecki's inflation, or there will be very costly trade-offs. While the costs of inflation are often exaggerated, high inflation economies are absolutely not beacons of stability and well-being.

There is also a very strong policy reason for not bringing back inflation. In a heavily regulated and uncompetitive economy, such as prevailed in the 1970s, the idea that the government could follow the Keynesian recipe and print money in a recession to ease the pain was discredited. The result was always higher inflation and the unemployment rate rose. The result was *stagflation*, inflation and unemployment rising together. But having killed inflation on a structural level, these policies now work. You and I think they can be dramatically improved, but the evidence is overwhelming that in competitive, deregulated, developed economies, printing money to stave off deflation and prevent recessions is costless in terms of inflation.

MARK: That's a very strong claim and sounds similar to some of the ideas held by a number of US economists who advised Bernie Sanders and known as modern monetary theory (MMT). They argue for aggressive fiscal spending given structurally low inflation.

ERIC: In the absence of inflation, it is true that we have a great deal more fiscal and monetary flexibility. MMT economists don't have a credible explanation of why inflation is dead. Hyman Minsky, their intellectual forefather, was completely wrong about inflation. Ironically, some of their policies might undermine price stability and end up limiting fiscal flexibility as a consequence. As you argued so forcefully in your book *Austerity*, and which has since become the consensus, aggressive fiscal and monetary stimulus should be used to counter recessions. But when the resources of the economy are fully employed, increasing the role of government requires resources to be taken from somewhere else. MMT often gives the impression there is a free lunch. In recessions, there is, but at times of full employment, there isn't. MMTers typically either talk as if this is not the case, or they revert to a Panglossian view of state intervention. I think we need a more innovative and rigorous framework for using the state's balance sheet to address wealth inequality and climate change.

MARK: To me, economics is only part of the issue. If we are in a deregulated, competitive and globally-interlinked world, and it is hard to generate inflation, then the "crowding out" of resources should be less of a problem. Indeed, the MMT answer to inflation is to raise taxes. But for me that raises a question of politics. Who votes for higher taxes and then wins at the ballot box? And who thinks that the idea of "the government" planning the investment that we all supposedly agree upon (we don't, for better or ill) is not a major political issue? Finally, income and wealth taxes, it should be remembered, were brought into the world not just to fight inflation or to raise revenue, but to fight plutocracy. I'm a bit worried about a theory of the economy that wants to give those with all the assets even more while promising to tax them even less so long as there is no inflation. But we digress, let's get back to the main point – that the control of inflation has brought huge benefits, and in addition we need strong financial systems. What else needs to be fixed?

ERIC: Clearly, if Trump and his coterie decide to deregulate the financial sector again, America will run the risk of calamity. But at a global level, people have not forgotten 2008 and its lessons. The global financial regulators are determined to keep the banks reined in and heavily regulated. But apart from banking there are three major challenges for which we need new code. The first we have already spoken about at length, inequality.

Even with my caveats about measurement, inequality has been a problem since the 1980s, and it has been largely ignored since the 1980s too. Almost everyone now agrees that we need to do something about extremes of wealth and income inequality – the legitimate face of angrynomics. Bill Gates thinks it's gone too far. Even Warren Buffett, who if he doesn't die, will end up owning almost everything, thinks it's gone too far.

It's a serious problem for a host of reasons we have already spoken about. But new research is showing us how it exacerbates health inequalities, restricts social mobility and undermines democracy.[29] Taxes are one answer, of course, not least because by taxing a relatively small share of the income of the very wealthy and giving it to those on low incomes we can make a big difference to the lives of those living in insecurity, and the top decile will barely notice. Indeed, public opinion in much of the developed world seems to be turning very much in this direction.[30] And as you mentioned a moment ago, it's worth remembering that in the US case, taxes were introduced to tame plutocracy at the end of the nineteenth century as much as they were brought in to raise revenue.

Indeed, the extremes of wealth inequality we are witnessing today are also producing moral outrage just as political corruption and gratuitous excess did back then. But we need to go beyond taxes that the super-rich and their paid-off politicians will fight against tooth and nail as the reaction to Senator Warren's wealth tax proposals in the 2020 US election campaign show clearly. We need a more positive angle to attack inequality and its ills and the key to that is to support everyone else's consumption and income through the broader ownership of assets.

By providing ownership of assets to those who have very few or even none we can insure against the change and risk that is built into our economy. Our new software needs to address wealth inequality so that our societies become more adaptive to change, and a broader asset ownership is key. And by that I mean something way more than Margaret Thatcher's famous "property-owning democracy". We need fundamentally new ideas about who owns what and who gets the returns to assets.

The second more technical problem is low interest rates. This is partly a legacy of v.3.0's success in controlling inflation, but it is also a consequence of demographic change and high private sector debt levels. The problem posed by close-to-zero interest rates is that central banks are impotent in the face of an economic shock that threatens recession. If interest rates are already so low, cutting interest rates and buying bonds is pointless. Given this, we need to give central banks new tools which are fairer and more effective. In my view the narrative among economists on this issue has been far too defeatist and pessimistic. Close-to-zero interest rates actually creates a huge opportunity to tackle both wealth inequality and climate change. The problem with both these issues is not resources – it's ideas.

You and I, together with a growing group of economists across the world, have already devised new tools, which we will discuss in a moment, sometimes bracketed under the unhelpful moniker of "helicopter money". This involves transferring cash to households to support consumption. But we have also outlined how a system of dual interest rates could be harnessed to turbocharge investment in sustainable initiatives. Movements such as Extinction Rebellion and Kate Raworth's *Doughnut Economics* are right to demand a greater sense of urgency. What has been lacking is a simple non-zero-sum solution. I firmly believe that protecting the environment is a huge opportunity for economic regeneration.

MARK: Okay, so we need to fix three things. First of all, the control of inflation and heavily regulated banks are prerequisites. No inflation means we can print money to stave off recession, but with interest rates close to zero and debt levels so high central banks need new tools to get that job done if they need to next time around, as they surely will. We can discuss how to do this. Secondly, we also want to radically address wealth inequality. We think we can do this without relying on raising taxes, or pursuing long-shots like global cooperation over the hidden wealth of oligarchs or on new wealth taxes, as proposed by economists around Senator Elizabeth Warren, for example. Thirdly, we want to finance a boom in sustainable investment that really begins the effort to decarbonize our economies. We can then use all of these policies to mitigate micro-stressors and empower individuals.

Let's start with one of the most innovative of these policies: a National Wealth Fund to tackle inequality. Before we do so however, it's worth outlining what a measure of good policy is. Too many of the solutions on the table – like a global wealth tax – are non-starters from a tactical political standpoint. I get irritated about policy discussions that focus on what is "optimal". We need to prioritize what is *effective*. The idea of global wealth taxes, or even aggressive inheritance taxes on those holding assets in excess of say $5 million or even $50 million, are very tough political challenges, no matter how "right" they are as technical solutions, and even if US public opinion has recently been shifting in that direction. The rich are powerful and there is a global tax avoidance industry that governments everywhere seem reluctant to call out. So, to go back to our earlier analogy, how do we write new code to get us out of this mess? What does a smart policy look like?

ERIC: A smart policy has to have three features. First, it has to make a big difference. Second, it should be simple and explainable. Third, it should cut across traditional political lines such that it garners and keeps support across electoral cycles. If it has those three features, it can allow a new politics that calms the anger. It works, it's sellable, and there is no reason to oppose it. So, let's start with our first serious hardware modification – a national wealth fund (NWF) to tackle inequality.

MARK: The challenge we set ourselves is simple. We want everyone in the economy to have assets that generate income. Why should a big inheritance, or a trust fund, be the purview of the rich? In most of the developed world the top 20 per cent of the population owns more than 80 per cent of the assets. And as we established, there is a strong and regressive intergenerational component to this too. Reasonable people think it would be great to redress this balance. The poorest 20 per cent inherit and own very little indeed. The old idea was to use taxation. This fails two points of our three-point test. While it works, there is huge political opposition to tax raises and capital is global – it's too hard to catch. So, we need a different fix. So let's try national wealth funds.

First off, we know building a NWF is feasible because *sovereign* wealth funds already exist. Places like Singapore, Norway, many of the Gulf States – not exactly typical Marxist enclaves – have these institutions. Sovereign wealth funds are large holdings of international assets – bonds, stocks, infrastructure and property – which the state owns and either manages itself or mandates third parties to manage on its behalf. Now it is important to be clear that the state is not trying to run these assets – this is not old-school nationalization. The assets in sovereign wealth funds are traded on global exchanges, and these sovereign wealth funds are typically passive minority holders of these assets. In the same way that large charities hold investment assets, or pension funds, or university endowments, like Harvard, sovereign wealth funds are buying assets to accumulate savings and wealth on behalf of their public from the earnings such assets accrue. Now Singapore, the Gulf States and Norway are an odd group of countries. Can we copy them? Do we want to?

ERIC: Yes, and no. Let me explain. The origin of these wealth funds is typically a very large balance of payments surplus (these countries export lots more than they import and have to bank the receipts or send them abroad to earn an income with them), which creates a financial dilemma for these states. A country that is an oil producer, or simply an extremely successful exporter like Singapore, can respond to a huge trade surplus either by allowing their exchange rate to strengthen – which could damage other parts of their economy – or it can use the foreign currency it receives to accumulate assets on behalf of the state, which is what these countries have done. Our twist is to do this without large balance of payments surpluses. We think we can do this by taking the upside of the financial crisis – there is one! – along with the help of global demographic trends and low inflation.

One of the things that has happened since the 2008 financial crisis is that the government is able to borrow at a negative real interest rate. That means that the private sector is actually paying the government to borrow. Can you imagine a world where you take out a mortgage and the bank actually pays you for having the mortgage? Who wouldn't do that?

And that's the world we currently inhabit. The bizarre thing in this context, is that instead of governments capitalizing on this collapse in their cost of finance, we have seen the opposite – central banks handwringing over how low interest rates are, and governments adopting "austerity" policies. This is economic illiteracy.

So let's think this through. In Germany, France, and the UK, for example, the government can issue 20–30-year bonds at negative real interest rates. The US 10-year treasury bond is similarly on a negative yield, after inflation. This is analogous to striking oil. Here's why.

Let's say the UK government issues 20 per cent of GDP in 15-year gilts (bonds) at a zero real interest rate – to keep the maths simple. In 15 years, the real value of the debt is unchanged. Now if the proceeds are invested in a diversified basket of global equities, which are currently priced to deliver 4–6 per cent real returns, the value of the assets will more than double in real terms over the same period. The fund would have a *net* asset value equivalent to 20 per cent of GDP.

The existence of negative real interest rates for the government is like discovering oil. It is a source of wealth. The surplus generated every 10–20 years in this way could be distributed in the form of individual trust funds to the 80 per cent of households who own the fewest assets. These trust funds could be drawn upon for specific earmarked uses, such as housing, education and healthcare, and business start-ups.

MARK: You and I have been writing about this idea since the financial crisis, including an article in the *Harvard Business Review*, and there is now a growing literature on the subject of creating national wealth funds.[31] What is distinct about what we are proposing?

ERIC: There are two distinct features. Firstly, we are exploiting a unique feature of the world today: negative real interest rates. It is absurd that governments are not taking advantage of this. The only reason a very large national wealth fund can be created quickly is because the cost of debt to the government is so low. This is part of the solution to secular stagnation. The second distinct feature of what we are proposing is distributing ownership to those who don't have assets. We want to create a national inheritance that goes beyond national insurance.

MARK: This is compelling. It could be set up and implemented in a matter of months. It's prudent because although the government is issuing debt its *net* debt, the difference between its assets and liabilities – which is what really matters – is unchanged because the government is not issuing debt to spend it on consumption. It's buying real assets with it. And we only distribute a surplus, after the debt has been repaid, in 10–15 years, depending on the success of the investments. The returns generated by existing sovereign wealth funds suggest a very high probability of success. But let's address three typical concerns. First, this sounds risky: issuing debt and buying stocks. Second, doesn't the government already have too much debt? Third, why is the government able to do this? It sounds too good to be true. If interest rates rise will it no longer be possible?

ERIC: There's a simple answer to these questions, and a more technical one. I'll give the simple answer first. Imagine that your bank offered to pay you to take out a mortgage. Instead of charging you interest, you get paid 1 per cent. So, you take out a mortgage, purchase a property, and rent it out, with a rental yield of say, 6 per cent. Each year you therefore make a 7 per cent return (6% in rental income, and 1% which the bank pays you), and this compounds over time. In ten years you can repay the mortgage and own the rental property outright. This may seem too good to be true, but these are the consequences of compound interest and the government's cost of capital. It's an interesting question as to why this is the case, why the private sector is willing to lend to the government at a zero or negative real return. I'll come back to this. But the first point to stress is that given the government's current real cost of debt, any investment it makes with positive real return creates value for the state.

Let's address the point about risk. There *are* risks involved – which isn't a reason not to do something – but it's important to be clear about the nature of these risks. In the rental property example, you could be unlucky – the property gets flooded, or destroyed in an earthquake. You don't get any rental income, the value falls, and you still have a debt to repay at the end of the term. What then are the risks to a government that issues bonds at zero real interest rates and buys a diversified portfolio of global assets, yielding 4–6 per cent?

The global stock market is a claim on the capital stock of the world – Europe, China, Japan, the rest of Asia and North America. For this to go badly wrong you would need to see serious damage to the capital base of the entire world. All the evidence suggests that it is growing, not shrinking, and if you invest for periods of 10–20 years, you can look through periodic crashes, when people panic, and pick-up bargains along the way to add to the portfolio, which is broadly what most of the sovereign wealth funds have done.

To seriously impair this wealth fund you would need to have a world war or a global economic catastrophe and not just a cyclical stock market crash, from which the fund could actually benefit. So yes, there won't be much to distribute if there's a major war or a meteor destroys the global economy, but in either of these scenarios a wealth fund's losses will be the least of our worries.

MARK: Given that the probability of failure is very low, this is a very sensible policy for governments to pursue. It isn't ideological. Indeed, ownership for everyone should be a bipartisan issue – and it addresses a critical component of angrynomics. Now, let's briefly get technical. Why *is* the government able to borrow so cheaply, and why might it be uniquely positioned to exploit the excess return that it can generate from buying private-sector assets?

ERIC: There are two forces at work that have created this unforeseen opportunity. The first are the demographic trends that we have discussed. The second is an unintended consequence of a world of very low inflation – government bonds have become insurance policies for the private sector. These two factors have caused the cost of borrowing by the state to collapse. In the rich developed world, we have an aging population with a concentrated ownership of assets. Old people tend to be risk averse, with very visible liabilities, such as pensions, medical, and care needs. All of the forces you have described in our discussion of private stressors have resulted in a very strong propensity to save, and therefore there is a very high demand for government bonds which have become, in essence, savings bonds.

MARK: Okay, I get that. A lot of very risk averse old people and their pension managers are buying government bonds with very low real returns because they want certainty – even if they will lose money after inflation. But what about this second point – that the state can borrow at very low interest rates because government bonds are *insurance policies*. What does that mean?

ERIC: What you and I have suggested – which I think is innovative – is that we could exploit the fact that the cost of capital of the government appears to be negatively correlated with the cost of capital with the private sector.

MARK: Okay, in plain English, what does that mean?

ERIC: When a firm issues equity in the stock market, it gives away a share of its profits and ownership. Now what happens in a recession? In a recession, profits fall, and when profits fall there is a risk that companies may go out of business. If I am a private company in a recession and seeing my profits falling, in order to raise finance I have to give away a larger share of my business. The power in such a situation is with the investor buying the shares. And this is reflected in the behaviour of stock markets. Stock markets fall in recessions, with remarkable reliability. The US stock market typically falls 50 per cent during a recession.

In other words, the cost of financing for private-sector capital is cyclical. In good times, when the economy is growing, people have jobs, and corporate profits are strong, stock markets typically rise, and companies can issue shares at reasonable prices. Investors will still demand 6–7 per cent real returns because they worry a recession might be around the corner, but all is well. During a recession, profits fall, people get fired, and stock prices typically collapse. But the interesting thing is that in a world of low inflation, the cost of financing for governments does the complete opposite. Why? *Because the government finances itself at the rate of interest, and because interest rates fall in a recession, the government's cost of debt collapses.*

As a consequence, it is frequently the case that the returns to investing in the private sector are elevated when the government's cost of financing is low. So, the government is able to issue bonds at a very low yield, and buy equities with a high return. This is currently the case in Europe, the UK and Japan.

During the Asian crisis recession in 1998, the Hong Kong Monetary Authority invested US$15 billion in the Hong Kong stock market to offset the panic in the private sector. At the time it was widely criticized by commentators for undermining faith in Hong Kong's market-based system. Yet far from doing so it helped stabilize the system and ended up generating an astronomical return for the state. Let's learn that lesson and apply it. We should build equity-driven national wealth funds that act in this way as a matter of policy. Funds that redistribute the excess return in the form of broader asset ownership. In contrast to wealth taxes, this is a voluntary process insofar as the government is not taxing to redistribute, so there should be less political resistance, and indeed much support.

MARK: This is really important. We seem to have identified a feature of v.3.0 that allows us to tackle in a serious way one of the legitimate grievances of angrynomics – extreme wealth inequality – one that the system itself generates, without raising taxes. And we can create perhaps as much as 20 per cent of GDP in wealth every 15 or so years for those in our society who don't have assets. Asset ownership is, as you say, a form of insurance. If you have a pool of assets to draw down for health, education and training, you have protection against some of the most expensive and important needs that households face.

As such, a NWF would address some of the legitimate anger against wealth inequality generated by angrynomics along with mitigating the private stressors of uncertainty about health, education and housing. Who can object to that?

ERIC: Okay, that's a good start, a viable powerful policy that could make a serious difference to people's lives and one that addresses the concentration of wealth in society. Let's now shift to the issue of income. The idea of a universal basic income (UBI) – a minimum level of income paid to all citizens – has gained a lot of traction recently. The two major objections to it are, firstly, how do we pay for it without undermining the resources available for social security, and secondly, is it right for people to receive something for nothing? We have proposed a twist on UBI which avoids these objections – a data dividend.

MARK: Rather than pay people something to do nothing, which is a typical objection, we're suggesting we should get paid for something that is already ours. We want to grant private-sector firms the right to access our data, but for a fee, and that could in part fund a minimum income.

ERIC: There are a number of important issues here. Personally, I am very happy with tech firms and financial institutions having access to my data. I can see huge benefits, from medical diagnosis using AI, or Amazon suggesting to me what I want before I know about it. I want to access these productivity gains. I'm not hung up on privacy. But I also realize that there are scale economies in a lot of these businesses, and therefore recognize that some of them may tend towards monopoly. Certainly, Google, Facebook, Amazon and Apple have monopolistic characteristics. Typically, monopolies are either state-owned or state-regulated, otherwise their market power is open to abuse to the detriment of the consumer. For example, we appreciate that we can only have one railway line, but that we can't allow a private firm operating it to charge whatever fare it wants – so we regulate it. Big tech has similar features.

MARK: Talk me through how a data dividend might work.

ERIC: Well, one idea you and I are working on, is that the government could license data. Because the dominant tech firms – Apple, Amazon, Facebook and Google – are using our collective data as the basic fuel for their profit engines, there is a deal to be struck.

In return for access to our data, we can either ask them to pay a royalty, a one-off payment, or we could grant a data "licence" for 30 or 40 years in the same way as the digital spectrum was auctioned to mobile phone companies. This could be done at a national level. One possibility would be to invest the proceeds from this licence fee or royalty in the shares of these companies and pay out an equal dividend to everyone who grants them access to their data. That is not something for nothing. This is a royalty payment reflecting a property right. The proceeds from data licences are unlikely to be enough on their own to create a dividend stream sufficient to create a minimum income of, say, $12,000 per adult citizen, but it would be a start. I also think a very low initial minimum sum, as a trial, could make a big difference to many people's lives, and could be an easier sell politically – particularly if the effects are very positive.

MARK: Why don't we just use the tax system? Why don't we just get them to pay their taxes and increase our social and infrastructural investments? Take the example of Amazon expecting a $2 billion tax pay-off for simply opening up shop in New York while paying zero taxes in 2017![32]

ERIC: We could do, but we aren't, and we won't. It's worth thinking about this in the context of our three requirements of good ideas: make a difference, keep it simple, cut across political lines. We are suggesting that property rights be established and that monopoly data licences be auctioned. We are then paying the dividends to the people who volunteer the data. That's an ownership-based, fair solution. But there's another twist. The behaviour of the big tech companies is very poorly understood. As we discussed in Dialogue 4, some of them, like Amazon and Facebook, are aggressively competing with other companies, and in doing so they are providing consumers with services for free, as in the case of Facebook, or at ever-lower prices, as in Amazon's case. We don't want to prevent them from doing that. We want to encourage them, but we want them to share the gains more broadly.

Apple, for example, has huge profit margins and sells phones at premium prices, and so in one sense, they are ripping everyone off. But if we own their equity we don't really mind. They pay out great dividends to their shareholders – and that could be all of us in a NWF – and we would then have some income from them from the data dividend too. If Amazon on the other hand uses our data to attack one industry after another, we don't mind either – we will make large capital gains as it grows, and we benefit from lower prices of goods and services. Should Amazon become a huge monopolist paying out huge dividends, we would be part owners and dividend receivers. And if it eventually tries to rip us all off as a monopolist, it's much easier to regulate something in which you have a big ownership stake. This is why the data dividend could be

143

more attractive than a simple UBI. It provides us with an opt-in income, but it also addresses the issue of tech monopolies and data ownership.

MARK: If I were to create a hierarchy of sins revealed by angrynomics, top of the list is creating recessions. The euro crisis is the most legitimate source of public anger I can think of – the needless and profound destruction of large parts of the economies of Italy, Spain, Portugal and Greece. It is no coincidence that the voices of angrynomics are loudest in Europe. The euro crisis, as we have both documented, was reprehensible. There's a genuine case for taking the policymakers to court and trying them at a human rights tribunal. What was done to Greece, Portugal, Spain and Italy is unforgivable. And the human suffering needlessly caused is profoundly destructive. Even after ten years, the recovery was not complete.

We know how to end recessions in a low inflation world, and it is doubly unforgivable when there is no inflation. If you have inflation, there may be a trade-off. It may have been reasonable in the 1970s to say that to control ever-rising inflation we needed higher unemployment – you can debate that. But that is not where we are today. Deflation is now a greater risk in economic downturns than inflation. If that is the case, there is absolutely no reason why there should be long-lasting recessions, for the very simple reason that to solve it you can give people money. It is as simple as that.

In any well-ordered society, to use a Rawlsian phrase, with the ability to print money, the central bank can create spending on demand. Given this, there should never be long-lasting or severe recessions in economies with very low inflation. Recessions are caused by people not spending enough. We wouldn't worry about recessions if everyone had enough money to pay their rent, buy food, pay their bills and educate their children. The reason we care about recessions is because people want to spend more money than they can. The question is then simply this: how do we give them more money to spend?

The approach up until now has been that when a recession hits, we try to boost spending by lowering borrowing costs, so companies can borrow to invest, and households can borrow to spend, and in doing so we have encouraged the private sector to load up with debt. In practical terms, a lot of this was about handing cash to people.

Think of the UK where a large share of the mortgage market was based on variable-rate mortgages, or adjustable-rate mortgages as the Americans call them. As soon as the Bank of England cuts interest rates for many households their disposable income immediately goes up. They are handing you money. It's just done in a non-transparent way and it can only work when you have high interest rates. But that no longer works anymore because we have reached the point where the interest rates are close to zero. Banks are saying that rates are now so low that they can't pass on cuts to households, while borrowers are saying "have you seen how high our debts are?" We need to rethink all of this.

ERIC: You and I wrote a piece on what some folks call "helicopter drops" in *Foreign Affairs* in 2014, and we've talked about it for as long as we've known each other. It has become much more broadly accepted as an idea among the mainstream economics profession and even among some central banks. The simple version is that we give central banks the power to transfer money directly to households. Very encouragingly the Czech central bank, one of the world's most successful, pre- and post-crisis, has written an academic paper presenting empirical evidence to show that this would work. Senior officials there have also suggested that it's on the table if a recession hits again.

There is a lot of confusion, not least among economists about so-called helicopter drops. The name hasn't helped. Many get hung up on how to define it, rather than how to do it. The Czech paper is refreshingly to the point. They have a very clear name for it, *direct support for consumption*. That's what we are advocating. We don't really care what it's called, but let's give central banks the power to transfer cash to households. And if central banks already have the power – which arguably the European Central Bank does – all they need to do is clearly explain how they will use it next time a recession strikes.

MARK: We've said that you can cut interest rates, but that's not working. You can also do what is called quantitative easing (QE), that is, you buy all the assets you can – bonds and stocks and other assets – and in so doing you boost their prices. This creates a "wealth effect" whereby because people with assets see gains, they feel richer and spend more money, and we hope that eventually that impacts on the wider economy as it trickles down to everyone else. Now here's how inefficient that is – by analogy. Imagine you want a cup of tea. You go into the garden and you get the garden hose, you stick it in the letterbox. Then you run around and go in the back door, take the lid off the kettle. You run out again, shut the doors and turn on the garden hose. And you just flood the house with water. Now, eventually some will get in the kettle. We're saying, "just put some water in the kettle!"

ERIC: Exactly. You have a simple problem, which is that people aren't spending enough. You can jack up asset prices to try and make them feel better, you can buy assets way above their true value from a tiny minority of the population and hope that spills over, or you could just give everyone £1,000 or $1,000, and do it every quarter, until we're at full employment and inflation hits target. By definition, at that point, the recession is over and then you can raise interest rates and stop handing out the cash. And it will be cheaper than QE. Given where we are structurally with interest rates, I believe that this is an idea that one nation state will eventually adopt, perhaps it will be the Czech Republic, and it will work. There will be a positive contagion of ideas and we will all wonder why we didn't do it sooner.

A lot of people try to counter our proposal that central banks should have the power to transfer cash to households in direct support of consumption, by asking, "do central banks have the legitimacy to do this?" I really don't get this. We can legislate the mandate of the central bank. We either grant them the legitimacy to do this, or encourage them to use their existing mandates. The ECB can already do this within the scope of its mandate. It has a legal requirement to maintain price stability, and pretty much has free rein by law on how to achieve this, as long as it keeps national treasuries out of things.

Under its programme of TLTROs (don't ask!), the ECB can in fact make perpetual zero-rate loans to all eurozone citizens to combat deflation. The programme could be administered by commercial banks in the same manner as current TLTROs. This would work well. When we first raised the idea of perpetual TLTROs in 2014, it fell on deaf ears. But encouragingly, when the eurozone economy was on the brink of recession again in mid-2019, senior establishment central bankers, including Stan Fischer, former deputy chairman of the US Federal Reserve, and the former president of the Swiss National Bank came out in support of perpetual loans to households as a policy response from the ECB.

The Bank of England and the Bank of Japan have similar lending facilities that could be used to make similar transfers, but it does not appear that under current US law the Federal Reserve would be able to do this. The ECB can do it legally, and probably most other central banks in the world can also. Is there anything else the US can do? Well, Ben Bernanke has suggested that the Fed could have an account at the US Treasury, and when interest rates are close to zero and it wants to provide a further boost to the economy, it just places cash in the account and says "here's $50 billion or $100 billion – go spend it or distribute it".

MARK: Okay, so we have turned what initially looks like a problem – the threat of deflation and zero interest rates – into an opportunity. The tools of central banking have been long due an overhaul. Some innovation by jurisdiction is required, but it can clearly be done. Central banks need to get cash into the hands of households instead of pursuing damaging experiments with negative interest rates.

Let's now discuss the second tool you've recommended that central banks should adopt, which could also be used to turbocharge investment in decarbonization and regional development: dual interest rates. What are dual interest rates, and how would they work?

ERIC: Dual interest rates would allow central banks to separately target the rate of interest savers receive on their deposits and the rate borrowers pay on their loans. The best way to explain the power of dual interest rates is to contrast it with the current policies of negative interest rates. The problem with negative interest rates is that the effect of lower rates nets to zero – as you said earlier. So yes, if interest rates go negative it is – in theory at least – great for borrowers (assuming banks pass on the negative rates), but terrible for savers. This has led some economists to suggest that there is a "reversal rate", a level of interest rates where further reductions become a restriction on spending and no longer act as a stimulus. It is highly likely that we have already reached this point. Negative interest rates cause huge problems for banks, which rather obviously makes them less likely to lend. Similarly, it makes savers spend less and save more.

By contrast, dual interest rates are win-win. If the central bank leaves deposit rates at zero, or say at 0.5 per cent, and this determines the money market rate which is the benchmark for deposits, savers are at least not being punished or are receiving a modest income. This is a huge improvement on the current negative "tax" on deposits. At the same time, to improve the lot of borrowers, the central bank lends to the banks at a steeply negative interest rate, conditional on the banks making new loans for productive investments by the private sector.

I have suggested, for example, that using its existing TFS scheme (the UK's equivalent of the ECB's TLTROs), the Bank of England could make 5-year loans available to UK banks at −2 per cent fixed interest rates, contingent on these loans being extended to the private sector at negative rates to fund investments in decarbonization such as wind energy. Wind power already accounts for as much as 25 per cent of UK energy generation – why not target 50 per cent or 75 per cent? Dual interest rates turn recession and low inflation into a huge opportunity to finance a boom in sustainable energy. My beef with Greta Thunberg is not with her ambition – it's with her fear. We can do this. It's a complete myth that we lack the resources to overhaul our economies. In fact, the economic system is crying out for it.

This dovetails nicely with our final policy proposal: an overhaul of fiscal policy. There are two aspects to this. The first is the idea of independent fiscal councils, which seeks to take the political antagonism and bickering out of fiscal policy, and decide in advance of recessions what we want to do with tax and spend. The second is a smart rule for how much the government should borrow. The public is rightly confused: if negative rates means that the government is being paid by the private sector to borrow, how can they have "too much debt"? Every time a fiscal rule is adopted governments seem to break them. We're simultaneously told there's way too much debt and a shortage of "safe assets", which are, in fact, government bonds. Can we really have a shortage and too much at the same time? Mark?

MARK: Let me start with the idea of independent fiscal councils, or more broadly the idea of committing in advance of recession to what the national treasury – not the central bank – will do. Claudia Sahm, the US economist, has a very interesting idea, similar to our proposal for central banks, where the US treasury would commit in advance to make payments to households if unemployment starts rising. I think this is a brilliant idea for the US, particularly as the Federal Reserve is more restricted than other central banks.

Simon Wren-Lewis and others, such as Tony Yates and Samuel Brittan in the UK, have argued that you could have an independent fiscal council tasked either to distribute the transfer from the central bank that accumulates in a deep recession, or to decide in advance on how to cut taxes and boost government spending in a way that counters recession.

In other words, let's have part of the treasury that has fiscal resources that can be employed counter-cyclically.

Now there's a lot of jargon here, so what does this actually mean? Well, if you look across the world in the immediate aftermath of 2008, there was a global consensus that fiscal stimulus works – you spend more and tax less as a government and the economy recovers, in effect giving more money to the private sector to spend. And this policy was pursued across the world.

In Europe, the problem was Germany's fear of other countries free-riding on its credit rating and building up debt that becomes a liability for them in the monetary union. Ironically, the people who were most efficient post-2008 were the Chinese. They stimulated to the tune of 12 per cent of GDP and provided around 60 per cent of global growth from 2009 through 2012. The Chinese did classic Keynesian infrastructure spending. We know this works. We simply need to depoliticize it and that's what the idea of a fiscal council tries to do. So instead of waiting for the next recession and having an almighty political bun-fight, let's set up a fiscal council now, debate the issues now and agree what we would do when it happens, so we are ready to go when it does.

ERIC: Okay, we now have a serious set of policies to consign recessions to the dustbin of history. Politicians and policymakers who fail us now have no excuse. These are the right responses to legitimate anger. But is there more we can do? For example, our proposal of dual interest rates to "fuel" a green investment boom is only ignited if our economies require further stimulus.

MARK: This brings us to our final proposal: a flexible fiscal rule which turns "secular stagnation" (low interest rates) to our advantage. Without getting too bogged down in the technical details, whenever a country has a significant amount of public-sector debt the most important variable in assessing the sustainability of its borrowing is the relationship of its cost of debt to growth in nominal GDP. As a rule of thumb, if a government can borrow at an interest rate lower than its average rate of growth in GDP, it doesn't need to worry about borrowing more.

Instead of mechanically targeting a stable debt to GDP ratio as is common practice across much of the world – or worse still target an absolute amount as some parts of the US political establishment want to do – governments should operate with a much simpler objective: to expand their borrowing whenever their cost of borrowing falls below nominal GDP growth. Conversely, they should raise taxes when interest rates are higher.

On this basis, the world has potentially huge fiscal resources. It is highly likely that the current negative real interest rate on government bonds is enduring, given its cause is demography, higher GDP per capita, risk aversion, a very long-run decline in real rates over several centuries, and very low inflation.

As with the national wealth fund, we are not advocating that this fiscal resource be squandered. Far from it. We want to create greater social wealth, tackle climate change and regional economic development. As a matter of simple financial arithmetic, if the return on investment exceeds the cost of capital, value is created. The government has a negative real cost of capital, and the return to a vast array of green investments is positive – and extremely positive if the social return is considered. You mentioned wind energy. We also need an accelerated investment in charging infrastructure for electric vehicles. In tandem, subsidies could be made available to hit targets of

60–80 per cent electric vehicle rates within a decade. The challenge for climate campaigners at this point is to elucidate the major investment priorities. The fiscal resources, much like the monetary firepower, are available.

ERIC: Let me round-up. We have some radical policies to eliminate recessions, significantly redistribute income and wealth, insure people against risk and economic change, and encourage risk-taking in a fairer society. And we have the means to finance a green revolution. We now need to see countries implement these policies, and when they work, others will copy. The political class copies. It seldom thinks.

Aristotle suggested that the opposite of anger is *play*, or if not its opposite, its antithesis. It's an astute observation. Anger typically implies seriousness of intent, even violence: "Don't joke with him, he's angry". Now one of your takes on the trend towards nationalism is decidedly playful and is the main reason I'm optimistic for the future. Tell me about your idea of the unexpected upside to nationalism.

MARK: Here's the basic problem, and here's how the return to and rediscovery of the nation can help. We know things are deeply wrong and many people are deeply angry, but people don't know what to do and don't trust the people who are in charge. Nor do people trust the pointy-headed experts that tell you what's wrong for two good reasons. Their track record is pretty appalling, and they are all on the right side of this run-up in inequality, so why should we believe they have our interest at heart? They all seem to like globalization so the default opposition becomes nationalism. So, here is a controversial thought. Nationalism itself is not inherently good or bad, despite usually having an ugly face; it is not in-and-of itself a bad thing.

Think about it this way. The whole rhetoric of globalization that went along with neoliberalism was about embracing
a post-nationalist, individualist cosmopolitan identity. We
were told that those old class and nation-based identities were
redundant, that they belong in the past. But, so does the global
cosmopolitanism of the current era. When it turns out that
global economics doesn't pay off for the vast majority of people
in a nation, they become local nationalists. Now if it's the case
that nationalism is there whether you like it or not, does the
nation as a unit provide any advantages for thinking about this
thorny question of what to do next? Let's think about Europe
again. Europe's problem is not just bad policy, the fact is that
the project is fundamentally flawed. Here's what I mean by this.

If the whole point of the EU was to stop Germany and
France from going to war by redistributing the property rights
over coal and iron ore, and then building everything else on
top of that slowly, then those at the heart of the EU have done
a pretty good job. And even with Brexit, if the European Union
ceased to exist tomorrow, are we really saying that all the
trading, commercial, personal relationships would cease to be,
and we would be back to hermetically sealed units like in the
nineteenth century? I find that hard to believe.

Now what that tells me is that what's more important than
the formal structure of the system are the so-called "second-
order interactions" among the components. Now if you look
at the way Europe is increasingly governed – one currency,
one central bank, one policy target, one set of policies for all
countries to follow – it flies in the face of everything we know
about system complexity. The reason Scotland looks different
to England and England to Ireland is because although they are
all feeding off each other in systemic ways they also all have
different strengths and weaknesses.

ERIC: In other words, we want economic diversity at a national level because diversity fosters innovation and we can copy success. It also gives us some protection against failure since it can be isolated more easily. We don't want to think nationalistically, because that is a very reductive and limited ideology. But we want to organize politically at a national, or even sub-national level, because smaller political entities can be more innovative and accountable. It is a lazy and destructive set of ideas that is purely focused on cultural identity, but the policy diversity that's provided by the nation state is potentially hugely advantageous. Intelligent human progress involves lots of experiments about how to organize things, happening at the national level, and you observe the ones that are working best – and then you copy it. The Czech central bank could provide an example which others copy.

MARK: What Europe has done since the introduction of the euro, is to try and take a giant clothes iron to politics and iron flat all those differences, while saying there is only one set of things you should do, and we should all converge toward those policies. It is a very nineteenth-century hierarchical mode of thinking. Nationalism does not need to be about fetishizing national identities. Indeed, we can break nations down even further into regional entities. Think about Germany. One reason Germany works is because regional governments have real authority. This is also, surprisingly, true of China.

China is a big unitary state run by communists. Actually, no, it's not. It may be run by commies, but it is not a unitary state. With 1.4 billion people you simply can't do that. When China addresses things like poverty reduction, or industrial upgrading, they don't say, "all the firms in China should do this" or "all states should implement these policies". Instead they set targets, send them to the regional authorities, and let them figure it out. Some will lie, some will get it badly wrong, but the more experiments you have, the more likely you will end up with three or four who have succeeded in upgrading their firms or reducing poverty. Then you work out what it is they've done and see if it can be repeated more broadly. If you think about it, that's the innovation process.

ERIC: We always tend to think – wrongly – about governments being command and control and markets being the dynamic part. This is where Mariana Mazzucato's work is very good. There is no reason for the two of them to work orthogonally. You can have dynamic policymaking, on an experimental basis, which is exactly what the dynamic process of innovation is. So, let's not say the state is an unmitigated disaster, and the return of the state is a horrible thing. In fact, if European states were smaller, and actually more independent and able to try different policy solutions, Italy would find its own way, France would find its own way, and Europe would be better off.

In closing, let me take that back to one of the debates we were having about macroeconomic policy. I would say one thing that makes me optimistic, is that we've all got the same problem. Inflation is stubbornly low, the policy response everywhere has been ever-lower interest rates and a corresponding rise in leverage with its associated problems, and everyone has similar dilemmas about the distribution of wealth and income. Now given that is a global problem, there has to be a good chance that one of these countries comes up with some innovative ideas. If you contrast Europe with Asia, Asia has 15 or 20 independent central banks. The probability that one of those might respond to the zero bound on interest rates by doing something quite innovative is quite high. And once that happens, good ideas might just spread. And then even the political classes might notice.

Conclusions: what's been said, what's not, and what we don't want to forget

We hope that these dialogues have been a useful and fun way to engage with these ideas. To make sure we are all on the same page as we leave the page, we now want to summarize the core arguments that we have made and also to acknowledge what we are not saying.

Our ambition in *Angrynomics* has been to provide a primer on why the world is the way it is today. We also wanted to do that in a way that neither patronises nor expects the reader to trudge through a scholarly treatise. We also wanted to keep it short. That has costs. Some people may find our analysis partial and our proposals underdeveloped. If so, they have misunderstood the point of the book. Our aim has been to introduce these ideas, not to seek to prove them or make the case that nothing else matters.

For example, we both agree climate change is the most important challenge facing humanity. Indeed, from that perspective what we are writing about is trivia. But we think our decision not to start and end with climate change as the defining issue of the moment is justified on the following grounds. If you don't first do something about the anger, about restoring "economics" over angrynomics, then you can forget about ever getting serious policies to address climate change. We will never get them off the drawing board for fighting among ourselves, while allowing our tribal instincts to obscure our judgements.

Similarly, some may think we give short shrift to cultural explanations of these same phenomena, and indeed we do. But we do so because our framework allows us to do something about the underlying causes of angrynomics. Starting and ending with culture does nothing. It's a counsel of despair. Once you have decided that half your country is made up of people who are entirely different from you, and therefore wrong, it can only end badly. We need to aim higher than castigation and moral superiority as ends in and of themselves.

Finally, we think we need a new politics. One of the great errors of v.3.0 was to think that politics was reducible to finding "the right policies". The obsession with positive sum "win-win" solutions blinded us to the fact that politics is inherently distributional. Some win, some lose, and when the majority consistently lose the gig is up. As the 2016 Clinton campaign showed, having a "policy for every problem" as a list of band-aids for society's ills convinces few. People need to have a politics to mobilize behind, not a list of micro-policies that make little difference, are difficult to explain, and reinforce political divides.

What we have outlined is very ambitious – a way to end recessions by supporting household income directly, a means to give those who don't have an inheritance a significant stake in our collective capital, and a data dividend so technology proves of financial benefit to all and not just a tiny minority of "winners". We hope this can serve as the basis for a new politics that goes beyond the tired ideas behind v.3.0.

A huge failing of the post-Cold War era, the so-called "End of History", was the emergence of a demotivating, anodyne politics, where technocrats on the left or simplistic ideologues on the right, thought they knew what was best for people. A simultaneous erosion of many of the institutions of civil society left an intellectual vacuum for tribalists to occupy. Reversion to the basest form of group identity has been emerging for decades. The wake-up call, post-2009, is that this has gone global and is being perfected by the Trumps, the Orbans, and the Farages. A motivating sense of collective purpose and legitimate anger has been lost.

Our goal has been to provide a narrative that gives clarity and insight into this trend. Anger is the arc that helps us make sense of it all, in contrast to vague generalizations about an incoherent populism. Anger has a surprisingly clear structure. Its different manifestations can be identified. Having examined and analyzed anger ourselves, it has changed the way we frame the politics around us. We hope you see things differently, too.

When we see anger the first question we ask is, what type? Is this reasoned legitimate outrage? And are there issues, such as environmental degradation, which people *should* be angry about? We want to harness moral outrage. We should be forced to listen to those who have been ignored. Anger can be a positive motivating political and social force. But when we see private anger, our lens shifts. We see stress, anxiety, uncertainty – people who need support with difficult and rapid changes in their environment.

When we see tribal energy being fueled for electoral gain, or to generate fear, we are alert to manipulation by media and politicians motivated by vested interests. The exploitation of deeply embedded and often irrational propensities to form groups and the tribal rage that can ensue is dangerous and challenges the values upon which humanity rests.

Our goal has been both analytical and political. We think we have a coherent explanation of where we've come from, and how to make sense of what's happening in today's world. Anger is everywhere to be seen and, now, understood. But a politics that can move people needs a shot in the arm. The left and right are bereft of ideas – a return to the economics of state ownership of the 1970s, or an attempt to ape city-states like Singapore, are, to us, obvious dead-ends. The centre as its been constructed for the past 50 years, can no longer hold.

Centrist politicians, like Emmanuel Macron in France, only win elections because no one turns out to vote. In the UK, the common response to an increasingly polarized political elite, distracted by tribal trivia, is that a new third party is needed. But what would it stand for? Where are the ideas that will change people's lives and for which people will fight for?

While we have disagreed over the causal role of wealth and income inequality in the story of how we got here, what we both agree on is that tackling inequality in wealth is a challenge that will motivate and change people's lives. Our analysis and proposals throws down the gauntlet to left and right – we've shown that it can be done, without taxing the hell out of everyone or bankrupting the state. So get on with it!

We also will not tolerate recessions and unemployment when there is no inflation. This is a failure of the mind. Conventional thinking is an unforgiveable basis from which to reject compelling reforms of fiscal and monetary policy, which would make huge differences to people's lives.

Finally, we have outlined how the challenge of a data monopoly, which is owned by all, can be shared and returned to rightful ownership. We can all benefit not just from the innovation, but from the economic value creation.

Armed with these proposals, our politics can be changed. If it doesn't, we should all get angry.

Postscript: angrynomics in a pandemic

In late March 2020, the Covid-19 pandemic pushed the world into lockdown just as the proofs of this book landed on our desks. We immediately wondered, as the pandemic began to unfold, if what we had to say was still of relevance. We are convinced that it is. The key themes of this book are that any society encountering patched-up macroeconomic crashes (like 2008), the ever-increasing daily stressors of an aging society beset with rapid technological change, and rising inequality, was one that would produce an angry anti-system politics. That public anger would manifest itself in legitimate moral outrage and the weaponized energy of tribes. Not only is that still true, it is especially relevant in the current moment.

It may seem that the pandemic has quietened the anger, simply by everyone being told to stay indoors. Even the US presidential campaign seems to have been put on hold. Indeed, opinion polls have found renewed faith in centre parties and in the opinions of (health) experts. Meanwhile, those denying the pandemic or weaponizing it for politics seem to be losing their standing. So far, so good. But given that the underlying stressors we've discussed in this book are still there we need to consider how they interact with the actions taken to halt the pandemic. Indeed, with unemployment rocketing up everywhere, that anger, under lockdown for the moment, is likely to come back with some new targets as a result of this crisis.

An early example of this was the anger of Bernie supporters in the US asking why the Federal Reserve can always find a few trillion dollars to support financial markets whenever it's needed, but their asks, for student debt forgiveness and universal healthcare, are always "unaffordable". Class advantage is in full display in the pandemic as seen in who gets a Covid test, where you can decamp to avoid the virus (Devon in the UK and the Hamptons in the US), and who can work remotely to maintain an income and who cannot. As we move forward under lockdown the wisdom of the immigration restrictions popular with populists will be tested as much needed food for cities lies unpicked in the fields due to a lack of immigrant labour combining with the lockdown. And if the health services of the developed economies survive this onslaught there will be justifiable anger over how ill-prepared we were to confront this pandemic. Angrynomics, like economics, may be under lockdown, but it has not disappeared. The challenge for policy now is to use this moment to address not just the immediate needs of the pandemic, but the underlying fractures we identify in this book. The good news is that some of this is actually happening. Perhaps for once we will actually turn this crisis into an opportunity.

With a speed neither of us could have anticipated, many of the policy proposals we put forward in this book have moved to centre stage. Countries from Hong Kong and Denmark to the United States and the United Kingdom, have decided that cash transfers to households are the best way to provide immediate assistance to families. The European Central Bank (ECB) has introduced dual interest rates aimed at supporting small and medium-sized enterprises (SMEs). The US and UK governments both announced proposals to take equity stakes in firms on life-support as a result of the collapse in economic activity. More broadly, the immediate consensus has been that the cash flow of households and companies needs to be supported at scale. Austerity has been thrown aside, without comment, even in Germany, which has announced a huge fiscal stimulus.

The main area of danger at the moment, despite this auspicious start, is the "how to" of policy. Most people agree that it would help if central banks could transfer cash to households, but they lack the means to do so. We have suggested that the ECB set up "perpetual zero-interest loans", which the banking system would administer for a nominal fee, and all European citizens could access. Former deputy chair of the Fed, Stan Fischer, and former head of the Swiss central bank, Philipp Hildebrand supported this idea in a paper published by the fund management firm, Blackrock.[33] But the infrastructure is not in place. That policy-makers did not foresee a pandemic coming is understandable, but it is an indictment of the policy-making community as a whole that they wasted a decade since the financial crisis without putting in place the recession-fighting infrastructure for monetary and fiscal policy. We knew a downturn was coming even if we did not know what form it would take.

One of our arguments for reform is that zero-interest rates, or even negative rates, do not signal the end of the efficacy of monetary policy. Far from it. Moving away from a reliance on a single interest rate should usher in an era of more intelligent central banking. We have outlined two dimensions. Cash transfers, as noted, are an obvious tool, and the infrastructure for delivering them should now – finally – be put in place. That the US is resorting to mailing out cheques at a time when phone/internet banking is commonplace is shocking, but given the lack of preparation, not surprising. The second dimension is through targeted lending and dual interest rates. We have argued that there are no limits to monetary stimulus if borrowing and lending rates can be separately targeted by central banks.

We saw the first examples of targeted lending being deployed by the Bank of England and the ECB. These organizations recognize that during the pandemic large, well-capitalized businesses will likely have reasonable access to funding through public markets and banking relationships, but that SMEs would face the most difficulty. They also provide large shares of employment. In order to mitigate against these effects both the ECB and the Bank of England redeployed existing direct lending schemes targeting SMEs.

In the ECB's case the interest rate on this round of TLTROs (targeted longer-term refinancing operations, which incentivize banks to lend by varying the rate at which they can borrow, depending on the area of the economy they are loaning to) has been made available at a rate below that at which the ECB remunerates bank deposits (reserves). This is the first case we are aware of where a central bank has explicitly introduced dual interest rates. The power of this remains under-appreciated. For example, if the ECB made 12-month loans to banks and required banks to extend these to SMEs, small firms would actually receive income payments. It is entirely reasonable to adjust the targets of such lending and dual interest rates depending on the nature of the shock. In more normal times we hope these tools are redeployed towards sustainable investments.

The institutional divergences we have discussed, particularly between the US and Europe, have again come to the fore.

Congress does have an ability to fall in line and deliver huge fiscal easing when it is needed, albeit with all the special interests looked after. But at least it gets there. Fiscal policy in Europe has again been incoherent and disorganized. At least the EU Commission has recommended a suspension of the absurdly restrictive fiscal rules, which was subsequently endorsed by the council of ministers. The Germans have even suspended their quasi-mythic budgetary "black zero" rule in order to respond to the pandemic. So there is progress.

At the ECB, after an initial faux pas at President Lagarde's first press conference triggered a minor panic in European government bond markets, the ECB stepped up and collapsed eurozone sovereign spreads with an "unlimited" commitment to quantitative easing (again). This combination of low yields underpinned by the central bank and a suspension of the fiscal rules, means individual countries across Europe have lesser fiscal constraints on their ability to borrow, which is still more constrained for some (Italy) rather than others (Germany). Hence the ECB's commitment to close spreads really matters if Italy is to respond effectively. Mutualized debt, a genuine new Coronabond, still seems beyond the pale at the time of writing, but the austerity snake oil does seem to have been finally thrown out – for the moment.

The great danger for Europe is to do "whatever it takes" during the crisis and then reach for the austerity lever as soon as it's over. That would be a re-run of the 2010–14 years, which crushed growth throughout Europe. Southern European unemployment still has not recovered from the last crisis. The pandemic will ensure it balloons to as much as 30 per cent. If Europe decides to squeeze budgets from that point, the anger generated will be uncontainable.

Another weakness is how to organize state support for the

corporate sector. We have proposed to policy-makers that rather than bailing-out bad management, a preemptive set of equity injections into strong companies within affected markets makes most sense. Moreover, if priced correctly and structured well, these assets should provide the seed capital for the debt-funded National Wealth Fund (NWF) we have proposed in this book.

Creating a public custodian for these equity shares solves multiple problems. It is often the case, for example, that in an emergency, the need to provide immediate support limits conditionality – what firms can do with the money they are given. For this reason, we have provided states with a template: inject equity, provide zero-interest loans, and take out warrants (options to buy more shares at a price agreed now). In doing this the state can provide plenty of liquidity for good businesses to survive the interruption, while ensuring it participates in the upside as these businesses recover and then grow. At the same time, by placing these assets in an NWF, with an independent board, a clear code of practice and rules prioritizing environmental and social governance, funds can be disbursed immediately, with conditionality and improvements in governance introduced on an ongoing basis.

Beyond these policy questions, the implications of the pandemic for the broader philosophical themes of angrynomics are starting to emerge. We have discussed the tension that exists between the nation state as an organizing unit of public policy, nationalism as a motivating ideology, and the global nature of many of our challenges – not least the environment. What we do not know yet is the extent to which the pandemic may result in a more extreme sense of isolationism, or if it draws nations together through a uniquely shared experience. Certainly it will be hard to argue that the state is powerless to change our societies when we are witnessing one of the largest concerted acts of state intervention since the Second World War.

There can also be little doubt that when we look back on this period the lens of moral legitimacy will play a significant part in determining how angry our collective response will be. Angrynomics has not disappeared with the crisis. The challenge that we face is to recognize that and to use our response to it to address the underlying fissures and fragilities in our societies that produce it in the first place. We have had a surprisingly good start. As Winston Churchill once opined, "when you find yourself going through hell, keep going". We hope that policy-makers who are currently on the right track heed that advice. How we respond to these challenges will likely determine how virulent a strain of angrynomics we will now face.

Further reading

We have deliberately written this book to be accessible and readable. As a result, we have sacrificed references to the many writers, thinkers and interlocutors who have contributed to our writing on these subjects. If you are new to these subject areas and this book has whetted your appetite, here is a selection of books and readings which we rate highly and that really got us going.

Anger is a subject that spans psychology, neuroscience, philosophy, political science and sociology. Most of the latest research is found in journal-based academic papers, but we recommend three books that are entirely accessible to the general reader and provide a fascinating introduction to the subject. The first is Martha Nussbaum's *Anger and Forgiveness: Resentment, Generosity and Judgement* (New York: Oxford University Press, 2016). Nussbaum, one of the world's leading philosophers, updates a perspective on anger, which dates back to Aristotle and which remains relevant and remarkably consistent with much more recent research in psychology and neuroscience.

The second is social psychologist, Carol Tavris's *Anger: the Misunderstood Emotion* (New York: Simon & Schuster, 1989), a wide-ranging take on the subject covering many aspects of both public and private anger. The third, written by one of the fathers of cognitive behavioural therapy, Aaron Beck, is *Prisoners of Hate: The Cognitive Basis of Anger, Hostility and Violence* (London: Harper-Collins, 1999). Beck simultaneously presents his own analysis of the origins of anger, provides fascinating historical and political case studies, and proposes thought-provoking and practical therapies for those at the frontline dealing with the consequences of anger and aggression. One of the challenges we have found in the literature on anger, in part because it spans so many fields, is that it lacks coherence and a shared typology. Often, it feels like very different phenomena are being analyzed. Our segregation of anger into four types – public, private, moral and tribal – is by no means complete, but does help us navigate and parse what we are interested in.

Much has been written about the emergence of "identity politics". Our focus has been to try and first understand why a loss of motivating political identity occurred in the first place. *Ruling the Void: The Hollowing-out of Western Democracy* (London: Verso, 2013) by political scientist Peter Mair, details the trends of disengagement and demotivation of the electorate in western democracies over the past 30 years, much of which chimes with our observations. Philip Coggan's brilliant book, *The Last Vote: The Threats to Western Democracy* (London: Allen Lane, 2013) is a more readable take on the threats to democracy, not least from the effects of money. Rounding out this section Edward Luce's *The Retreat of Western Liberalism* (London: Little, Brown, 2017) is a must read.

Political scientists have written an awful lot about political parties, but few have attempted to dissect how changes in the economy impact parties and party systems. One such attempt, which gives a good sense of how they link up, is Jonathan Hopkin and Mark Blyth, "The Global Economics of European Populism: Growth Regimes and Party System Change in Europe" (*Government and Opposition* 54:2 (2018), 193–225).

The economics profession has been engaged in a great deal of soul-searching since the financial crisis. The crisis revealed not just a failure of forecasting, but also a sense that the focus and methods of economic policy were out of touch – giving insufficient weight to climate change and inequality – and the conventional tools of analysis and policy needed a complete overhaul. Martin Wolf at the *Financial Times*, has provided deep insights through his columns on all of these issues. In two brilliant articles – "Why rigged capitalism is damaging social democracy" (*FT*, 18 September 2019) and "How to reform today's rigged capitalism" (*FT*, 3 December 2019) – he summarises both what is wrong and what should be done. Kate Raworth's *Doughnut Economics: Seven Ways to Think Like a 21st-Century Economist* (London: Random House, 2017) is a brilliant rebalancing of how economics should be done, putting true sustainability at its core. For a much less hopeful, but equally plausible account, see Branko Milanovic's brilliant *Capitalism, Alone: The Future of the System that Rules the World* (Cambridge, MA: Harvard University Press, 2019).

A huge amount has now been written about inequality. Thomas Piketty's masterpiece, *Capital in the Twenty-First Century* (Cambridge, MA: Harvard University Press, 2014) can take a lot of credit for this. But despite being a bestseller, and having influenced both of us in different ways, it is really a book for specialists – and if anything has provoked as much controversy as agreement, at least among economists. For an easier take on the issues around inequality, Tony Atkinson's *Inequality: What Can Be Done?* (Cambridge, MA: Harvard University Press, 2015) is superb. For a global picture, Branko Milanovic's *Global Inequality: A New Approach for the Age of Globalization* (Cambridge, MA: Harvard University Press, 2016) is unrivallled.

The effects of technology on our economies – beyond the obvious effects on our lives – are very unclear. Among the most insightful work is Erik Brynjolfsson's at MIT. Brynjolfsson and McAfee's *Race Against the Machine* (Digital Frontier Press, 2012) can be read in an afternoon, and is profoundly insightful, if rather overstated. A more measured account is given by the OECD's policy brief, "Putting faces to the jobs at risk of automation" (https://www.oecd.org/employment/

Automation-policy-brief-2018.pdf). The Roosevelt Institute's report, "Don't Fear the Robots" (https://rooseveltinstitute.org/wp-content/uploads/2018/06/Don%E2%80%99t-Fear-the-Robots.pdf) provides a still more sceptical view.

The greatest omission in the economics profession's response to the Global Financial Crisis is in the area of genuinely new policy proposals. That said, a consensus has started to build around our ideas of helicopter money, national wealth funds and dual interest rates. Martin Sandbu, again at the *Financial Times*, has written pithy and incisive articles on many of these issues, as well as an excellent new book, *The Economics of Belonging* (Princeton, NJ: Princeton University Press, 2020) whose arguments are quite in line with those made here. A reading list compiled by a search through his "Free Lunch" *FT* column is hard to beat.

For those unwilling or unable to pay for an *FT* subscription, Oxford professor, Simon Wren-Lewis, has blogged brilliantly on helicopter money and dual interest rates at his highly-accessible blog "Mainly Macro" (https://mainlymacro.blogspot.com/). The literature on national wealth funds has also proliferated. Roger Farmer has written brilliantly on the subject from a theoretical standpoint. Other notable work has been done by think tanks, most notably a detailed paper by Carys Roberts and Matthew Laurence, "Our Common Wealth: A Citizens' Wealth Fund for the UK" (https://www.ippr.org/research/publications/our-common-wealth). Our own work has contributed extensively to this debate, for example, see our "Print Less but Transfer More" (https://www.foreignaffairs.com/articles/united-states/2014-08-11/print-less-transfer-more) and "Fixing the Euro Zone and Reducing Inequality, Without Fleecing the Rich" (https://hbr.org/2015/01/fixing-the-euro-zone-and-reducing-inequality-without-fleecing-the-rich) as well as Eric Lonergan's blog "Philosophy of Money" (https://www.philosophyofmoney.net/blog/).

For those interested in the larger historical sweep in the middle of the book that is set up by the parable of the three economists, you may as well read the three economists in question. The first is Karl Polanyi's justifiably famous book *The Great Transformation: The Political and Economic Origins of Our Time* (Boston, MA: Beacon Press, 2002 [1944]). It's a social history of Britain, and by extension Europe, from the latter part of the eighteenth century through to the 1930s. The key idea is that of the "double movement", the attempt to turn social relations into commodity transactions produces a backlash against the market itself. The second economist mentioned is John Maynard Keynes. His book, *The General Theory of Employment, Interest and Money* (London: Macmillan, 1936) is not a ripping yarn by any stretch of the imagination, but it is a profoundly important work. If you can't face all of it start at Chapter 12 and go through to 18. That's the important bits. If you can't hack that, then try Chapters 4 and 5 of Mark Blyth's *Austerity: The History of a Dangerous Idea* (New York: Oxford University Press, 2015). The third economist mentioned, Michał Kalecki, is a much shorter read. His "Political Aspects of Full Employment", first published in the journal *Political Quarterly* in 1943 (https://onlinelibrary.wiley.com/doi/abs/10.1111/j.1467-923X.1943.tb01016.x) is just seven pages long. Here Kalecki explains why full employment capitalism will undermine itself and who will do the undermining. It's a piece that never ceases to amaze us.

Social scientists have long been interested in aging, but the effects of aging populations on the economy is a relative new area of research. For a wide-ranging critique of the baby-boomer generation Bruce Cannon Gibley's *A Generation of Sociopaths* (London: Hachette, 2017) and Steven Brill's less scathing but deeply penetrating *Tailspin* (New York: Knopf, 2018) are good places to start. For more technical work the US Federal Reserve has long been thinking about these effects, for example, Sheiner *et al.*, "A Primer on the Macroeconomic Implications of Population Aging" (https://www.federalreserve.gov/pubs/FEDS/2007/200701/200701pap.pdf) and Niklas Engbom, "Firm and Worker Dynamics in an Aging Labor Market" (https://www.minneapolisfed.org/research/wp/wp756.pdf).

On micro-level stressors in our daily lives, Elizabeth Anderson's *Private Government: How Employers Rule our Lives (and Why We Don't Talk about It)* (Princeton, NJ: Princeton University Press, 2017) is a great place to start. Then try Richard Wilkinson and Kate Pickett's *The Spirit Level: Why Equality is Better for Everyone* (London: Penguin, 2010) for an argument about the epidemiological effects of sustained inequality. Finally, Anne Case and Angus Deaton's paper "Mortality and Morbidity in the 21st Century" (https://www.brookings.edu/wp-content/uploads/2017/08/casetextsp17bpea.pdf) is a tragic indictment of how we cope with such stressors and the costs of doing so.

Notes

1. "We thought we were over that", *The Guardian*, Panama Papers Special Investigation, 11 April 2016; https://www.theguardian. com/world/2016/apr/11/we-thought-we-were-over-all-that-angry-icelanders-feel-like-its-2008-again?CMP=fb_gu.

2. "Testing theory: marginal product and wages", The FRED Blog, 29 August 2016; https://fredblog.stlouisfed.org/2016/08/ testing-theory-marginal-product-and-wages/.

3. "Will Brexit pollsters again help hedge funds make millions?", *Deutsche Welle*, 15 July 2019; https://www.dw.com/en/will-brexit-pollsters-again-help-hedge-funds-make-millions/ a-49518827.

4. Jonathan Hopkin & Mark Blyth, "The global economics of European populism: growth regimes and party system change in Europe", *Government and Opposition* 54:2 (2019), 193–225.

5. Ben Bernanke, "The Great Moderation", remarks at the Eastern Economic Association meeting, 20 February 2004: https:// www.federalreserve.gov/boarddocs/speeches/2004/20040220/.

6. See Mary O'Hara, "A journey to the sharp end of cuts in the UK", Austerity Bites; http://www.austeritybitesuk.com.

7. One recent and very large consequence was the way different age cohorts voted in the 2019 UK election; see: https://twitter. com/MkBlyth/status/1207430591622209537.

8. On the costs of the Brexit distraction see https://twitter.com/MkBlyth/status/1208317852018601984.

9. See, for example, "Anger motivates people to vote", Institute for Social Research, University of Michigan; https://isr.umich.edu/news-events/insights-newsletter/article/anger-motivates-people-to-vote-u-m-study-shows/.

10. See Eric Lawrence, John Sides & Henry Farrell, "Self-segregation or deliberation? Blog readership, participation and polarization in American politics", *Perspectives on Politics* 8:1 (2010), 141–57.

11. See Johannes Karreth, Jonathan Polk & Christopher Allen, "Catchall or catch and release? The electoral consequences of Social Democratic parties' march to the middle in Western Europe", *Comparative Political Studies* 46:7 (2013), 791–822.

12. O. Klimecki, D. Sander & P. Vuilleumier, "Distinct brain areas involved in anger versus punishment during social interactions", *Sci Rep* 8, 10556 (2018), doi:10.1038/s41598-018-28863-3.

13. Martha Nussbaum, *Anger and Forgiveness*, 20.

14. Dani Rodrik, "The inescapable trilemma of the world economy" (2007); https://rodrik.typepad.com/dani_rodriks_weblog/2007/06/the-inescapable.html.

15. Thiemo Fetzer, "Did austerity cause Brexit?", CESifo Working Paper Series, 7159 (2018), 5.

16. Board of Governors of the Federal Reserve System, "Report on the economic wellbeing of US households in 2017", 1; https://www.federalreserve.gov/publications/files/2017-report-economic-well-being-us-households-201805.pdf.

17. Board of Governors of the Federal Reserve System, FEDS Notes, "A wealthless recovery"; https://www.federalreserve.gov/

econres/notes/feds-notes/asset-ownership-and-the-uneven-recovery-from-the-great-recession-20180913.htm.

18. Anne Case & Angus Deaton, "Mortality and morbidity in the 21st century", *Brookings Papers on Economic Activity*, spring 2017; https://www.brookings.edu/wp-content/uploads/2017/08/casetextsp17bpea.pdf.

19. See Stephen Margolin & Juliet Schor, *The Golden Age of Capitalism* (New York: Oxford University Press, 1992).

20. See Eric Helleiner, *States and the Re-emergence of Global Finance* (Ithaca, NY: Cornell University Press, 1994).

21. See Juliet Johnson, *The Priests of Prosperity* (Ithaca, NY: Cornell University Press, 2016).

22. See "Citibank launches $100 million ad campaign"; https://www.marketingsherpa.com/article/citibank-launches-100-million-ad.

23. See Richard Wilkinson & Kate Pickett, *The Spirit Level: Why Greater Equality Makes Societies Stronger* (London: Allen Lane, 2009).

24. See respectively, Carl Frey & Michael Osborne, "The future of employment" (2013); https://www.oxfordmartin.ox.ac.uk/downloads/academic/The_Future_of_Employment.pdf; Bank of England, "Will a robot takeover my job"; https://www.bankofengland.co.uk/knowledgebank/will-a-robot-takeover-my-job and OECD, "Automation, skills use and training" (2018); https://www.oecd-ilibrary.org/fr/employment/automation-skills-use-and-training_2e2f4eea-en.

25. A search of the *Financial Times* archives from 2009 to 2020 on the topic "robots and employment" yields 403 results.

26. See Matthew Tracey & Joachim Fels, "70 is the new 65", Pimco (2016); https://www.pimco.com/en-us/insights/

viewpoints/in-depth/70-is-the-new-65-demographics-still-support-lower-rates-for-longer.

27. See Timo Fetzer, "Did austerity cause Brexit?" (2018), Warwick economics research papers series (WERPS) working paper 1170; http://wrap.warwick.ac.uk/106313/ and Sascha Becker & Thiemo Fetzer, "Does migration cause extreme voting?", CAGE Online Working Paper Series 306; https://ideas.repec.org/p/cge/wacage/306.html.

28. See Margaret Peters, *Trading Barriers: Immigration and the Remaking of Globalization* (Princeton, NJ: Princeton University Press, 2017).

29. See Philip Coggan, *The Last Vote: The Threats to Western Democracy* (London: Penguin, 2013).

30. See Frank Newport, "Americans continue to say U.S. wealth distribution is unfair", Gallup, 4 May 2015; https://news.gallup.com/poll/182987/americans-continue-say-wealth-distribution-unfair.aspx.

31. Eric Lonergan & Mark Blyth, "Fixing the euro zone and reducing inequality without fleecing the rich", *Harvard Business Review*, 9 January 2015: https://hbr.org/2015/01/fixing-the-euro-zone-and-reducing-inequality-without-fleecing-the-rich; Eric Lonergan and Mark Blyth, "Beyond bailouts", IPPR discussion paper, March 2020, https://www.ippr.org/files/2020-03/1585237065_beyond-bailouts-march2020.pdf.

32. See "New York dangled extra incentives in initial bid to lure Amazon HQ2", *Wall Street Journal*, 11 January 2020; https://www.wsj.com/articles/new-york-dangled-extra-incentives-in-initial-bid-to-lure-amazon-hq2-11578153600.

33. Elga Bartsch, Jean Boivin, Stanley Fischer & Philipp Hildebrand, "Dealing with the next downturn: from unconventional monetary policy to unprecedented policy coordination", SUERF Policy Note 105 (October 2019); https://www.suerf.org/docx/ f_77ae1a5da3b68dc65a9d1648242a29a7_8209_suerf.pdf.

Index

Note: **bold** page numbers indicate tables.

191

robotics *see* artificial intelligence
Rodrik, Dani 4, 39, 40
Russia 11, 41

Sahm, Claudia 150–51
Salvo, Francesca 87–8
Sandbu, Martin 174
Sanders, Bernie 128, 164
savings 93
scale economies 98, 99, 142
Scottish nationalism 7, 119
secular stability 125, 126, 127
service-based economy 52
Singapore 133, 134, 162
SMEs (small- and medium-sized
    enterprises) 164–5, 166
social democracy 63–4
social media 26, 27, 90, 98
Solow growth model 109
sovereign wealth funds 133–4
sovereignty 39
Spain 33–5, 38, 44, 45, 144
    protests against austerity in 85
spending
    increasing 145, 147, 151
    investment 40, 60
    power 145
    public sector 67, 70–71, 128, 151
    restrictions on 41, 44, 149
sports fans 8, 19–20, 21, 25
sports industry 99
stagflation 40, 74, 120, 128
status-injury 36, 54
stock markets 63, 137–8, 139–40
stress *see* anxiety/stress
strikes 73, 74
student loans 111
supply–demand 60, 96, 104
sustainable investment 131–2,
    149–50, 152, 153

Sweden 63–4, 72–3
Syria 111, 113

Tavris, Carol 36, 171
taxes 40, 50, 57, 108, 116, 124
    cuts in 34, 44, 111, 151
    dodging 2, 6, 20, 132–3, 143
    political opposition to 129, 130,
        132, 133
    raising 152
    on wealth 129, 130, 132, 140
Tea Party movement 85
technocracy 37, 42–3, 48, 160–61
technological change 29, 58, 96, 109
    and aging population 90, 106,
        122
    and competition 96, 97–8
    and dispersion of returns 97
    and fourth industrial revolution
        94
    further reading on 173–4
    and inequality 50, 53
    and labour market 102–104
    and media 24–5, 27
    as micro-stressor 88, 91, 94, 96,
        97–8, 99, 101–102, 105, 116,
        118
    and productivity 9, 10, 15, 105,
        122
    and rate of diffusion 14
    and uncertainty 101–102
telecommunications 96, 97, 142
terrorism 17, 18, 27
Thatcher, Margaret 75, 76, 118, 131
Thunberg, Greta 150
TLTRO programme (European
    Central Bank) 147–8
trade 21–2, 26, 42, 78, 154
    and neoliberalism 78
trade surplus 134